W9-BXY-756

Russia of
the Tsars

Titles in the World History Series

The Age of Augustus
The Age of Feudalism
The Age of Pericles
The Alamo
America in the 1960s
The American Frontier
The American Revolution
Ancient Greece
The Ancient Near East
Architecture
Aztec Civilization
The Battle of the Little
    Bighorn
The Black Death
The Byzantine Empire
Caesar's Conquest of Gaul
The California Gold Rush
The Chinese Cultural
    Revolution
The Civil Rights Movement
The Collapse of the Roman
    Republic
The Conquest of Mexico
The Crimean War
The Crusades
The Cuban Missile Crisis
The Cuban Revolution
The Early Middle Ages
Egypt of the Pharaohs
Elizabethan England
The End of the Cold War
The French and Indian War
The French Revolution
The Glorious Revolution
The Great Depression
Greek and Roman
    Mythology
Greek and Roman Science

Greek and Roman Theater
The History of Slavery
Hitler's Reich
The Hundred Years' War
The Industrial Revolution
The Inquisition
The Italian Renaissance
The Late Middle Ages
The Lewis and Clark
    Expedition
The Mexican Revolution
The Mexican War of
    Independence
Modern Japan
The Mongol Empire
The Persian Empire
The Punic Wars
The Reformation
The Relocation of the
    North American Indian
The Renaissance
The Roaring Twenties
The Roman Empire
The Roman Republic
Roosevelt and the New Deal
The Russian Revolution
Russia of the Tsars
The Scientific Revolution
The Spread of Islam
The Stone Age
Traditional Africa
Traditional Japan
The Travels of Marco Polo
Twentieth Century Science
The Wars of the Roses
The Watts Riot
Women's Suffrage

WORLD HISTORY SERIES ■ ■ ■

Russia of the Tsars

by
James E. Strickler

Lucent Books, P.O. Box 289011, San Diego, CA 92198-9011

JIM 1999

Library of Congress Cataloging-in-Publication Data

Strickler, Jim, 1956–
    Russia of the tsars / by Jim Strickler.
       p. cm.—(World history series)
    Includes bibliographical references and index.
Summary: Describes the history of Russia under the tsars, from
its beginnings before 1598 to the Revolution of 1917.
    ISBN 1-56006-295-9 (alk. paper)
    1. Russia—History—Juvenile literature.   [1. Russia—His-
tory.] I.Title. II. Series.
DK40.S895   1998
947—DC21   97-10876
                                             CIP
                                             AC

Copyright 1998 by Lucent Books, Inc., P.O. Box 289011,
San Diego, California 92198-9011

Printed in the U.S.A.

Contents

Foreword   6

Important Dates in the History of
    Russia of the Tsars   8

INTRODUCTION
Russia's Great Struggles   10

CHAPTER 1
Emergence of Russia: History Before 1598   12

CHAPTER 2
Growth of an Empire: 1598–1725   23

CHAPTER 3
The Reign of Catherine the Great: 1762–1796   36

CHAPTER 4
Russia's Resistance to Change: 1796–1856   44

CHAPTER 5
Reform and Reaction: 1856–1894   57

CHAPTER 6
The End of Tsarist Rule: 1894–1917   70

EPILOGUE
Russia Since 1917   80

Notes   85

For Further Reading   88

Additional Works Consulted   89

Index   92

Picture Credits   96

About the Author   96

Foreword

Each year on the first day of school, nearly every history teacher faces the task of explaining why his or her students should study history. One logical answer to this question is that exploring what happened in our past explains how the things we often take for granted—our customs, ideas, and institutions—came to be. As statesman and historian Winston Churchill put it, "Every nation or group of nations has its own tale to tell. Knowledge of the trials and struggles is necessary to all who would comprehend the problems, perils, challenges, and opportunities which confront us today." Thus, a study of history puts modern ideas and institutions in perspective. For example, though the founders of the United States were talented and creative thinkers, they clearly did not invent the concept of democracy. Instead, they adapted some democratic ideas that had originated in ancient Greece and with which the Romans, the British, and others had experimented. An exploration of these cultures, then, reveals their very real connection to us through institutions that continue to shape our daily lives.

Another reason often given for studying history is the idea that lessons exist in the past from which contemporary societies can benefit and learn. This idea, although controversial, has always been an intriguing one for historians. Those who agree that society can benefit from the past often quote philosopher George Santayana's famous statement, "Those who cannot remember the past are condemned to repeat it." Historians who ascribe to Santayana's philosophy believe that, for example, studying the events that led up to the major world wars or other significant historical events would allow society to chart a different and more favorable course in the future.

Just as difficult as convincing students to realize the importance of studying history is the search for useful and interesting supplementary materials that present historical events in a context that can be easily understood. The volumes in Lucent Books' World History Series attempt to present a broad, balanced, and penetrating view of the march of history. Ancient Egypt's important wars and rulers, for example, are presented against the rich and colorful backdrop of Egyptian religious, social, and cultural developments. The series engages the reader by enhancing historical events with these cultural contexts. For example, in *Ancient Greece*, the text covers the role of women in that society. Slavery is discussed in *The Roman Empire*, as well as how slaves earned their freedom. The numerous and varied aspects of everyday life in these and other societies are explored in each volume of the series. Additionally, the series covers the major political, cultural, and philosophical ideas as the torch of civilization is passed from ancient Mesopotamia and Egypt, through Greece, Rome, Medieval Europe, and other world cultures, to the modern day.

The material in the series is formatted in a thorough, precise, and organized manner. Each volume offers the reader a comprehensive and clearly written overview of an important historical event or period. The topic under discussion is placed in a broad historical context. For example, *The Italian Renaissance* begins with a discussion of the High Middle Ages and the loss of central control that allowed certain Italian cities to develop artistically. The book ends by looking forward to the Reformation and interpreting the societal changes that grew out of the Renaissance. Thus, students are not only involved in an historical era, but also enveloped by the events leading up to that era and the events following it.

One important and unique feature in the World History Series is the primary and secondary source quotations that richly supplement each volume. These quotes are useful in a number of ways. First, they allow students access to sources they would not normally be exposed to because of the difficulty and obscurity of the original source. The quotations range from interesting anecdotes to farsighted cultural perspectives and are drawn from historical witnesses both past and present. Second, the quotes demonstrate how and where historians themselves derive their information on the past as they strive to reach a consensus on historical events. Lastly, all of the quotes are footnoted, familiarizing students with the citation process and allowing them to verify quotes and/or look up the original source if the quote piques their interest.

Finally, the books in the World History Series provide a detailed launching point for further research. Each book contains a bibliography specifically geared toward student research. A second, annotated bibliography introduces students to all the sources the author consulted when compiling the book. A chronology of important dates gives students an overview, at a glance, of the topic covered. Where applicable, a glossary of terms is included.

In short, the series is designed not only to acquaint readers with the basics of history, but also to make them aware that their lives are a part of an ongoing human saga. Perhaps they will then come to the same realization as famed historian Arnold Toynbee. In his monumental work, *A Study of History*, he wrote about becoming aware of history flowing through him in a mighty current, and of his own life "welling like a wave in the flow of this vast tide."

Important Dates in the History of Russia of the Tsars

950	1000	1050	1100	1150	1200	1250	1300	1350	1400

988
Vladimir becomes a Christian.

1128
Famine hits Novgorod.

1223
Mongols invade Russia.

1462
Ivan III, the Great, takes power.

1487
Moscow conquers Novgorod.

1480
Russians formally throw off Mongol rule.

1533
Ivan IV, the Terrible, becomes ruler.

1580
Yermak's soldiers conquer Sibir.

1598
Time of Troubles begins.

1613
Michael Romanov becomes tsar.

1682
Peter I, the Great, becomes co-tsar.

1707
St. Petersburg becomes the capital.

1725
Peter the Great dies.

1762
Catherine II, the Great, becomes tsar.

1773
Pugachov begins his rebellion.

1801
Alexander I becomes tsar.

1812
Russians defeat Napoleon's army.

1825
Nicholas I becomes tsar; Decembrist Revolt fails.

1854
Crimean War begins.

Michael Romanov founded the Romanov Dynasty, which ruled Russia until 1917.

Cities like Moscow were the sites of much opposition to tsarist rule.

1855
Alexander II becomes tsar.

1856
Crimean War ends.

1861
Tsar Alexander II emancipates the serfs.

1881
Alexander III becomes tsar.

1891
Building of Trans-Siberian Railway begins.

1894
Nicholas II becomes tsar.

1904
Russo-Japanese War begins.

1905
Protesters killed on Bloody Sunday; Russo-Japanese War ends; mutiny occurs on the *Potemkin*.

1914
World War I begins.

1917
Russia pulls out of World War I; Nicholas II abdicates; Bolsheviks seize power.

1918
Nicholas II and his family are executed.

1922
The Union of Soviet Socialist Republics (USSR) is formed.

1939–1945
World War II.

Russia's Great Struggles

In the 1400s the country that became known as Russia was a small empire ruled from the city of Moscow. By 1917 the Russian Empire stretched from Poland in the west to the Pacific Ocean in the east, from the Arctic Ocean in the north to the Black Sea and China in the south. This enormous country was three times the size of the United States.

As Russia grew in size, its population grew in diversity. In the 1400s Russians were Slavs, a family of several ethnic groups in eastern Europe that speak related languages. Slavs include Russians, Poles, Ukrainians, Belorussians, and many other groups. By 1917 only about half of the people in Russia considered themselves ethnic Russians. The other half included various groups of Slavs as well as many non-Slavs. Among the largest non-Slav groups were the Uzbeks and the Kazakhs, who are closely related to the people of Turkey.

Russia's Poverty

While Russia was expanding and becoming more diverse between the 1400s and 1917, it remained a poor country under the rule of a dictator, called a tsar, or czar.

The tsars controlled the Russian government and considered the country to be their personal possession, given to them to manage by God. When a tsar died, another family member took power.

A small class of nobles served the tsar. They enforced orders, punished lawbreakers, and collected taxes. Some nobles belonged to rich, powerful families that

Russian tsars, such as Ivan the Terrible, held absolute power and considered themselves appointed by God to rule the country.

The majority of Russians were poor peasants who lived in small villages and who worked the land controlled by the government or nobles.

controlled tens of thousands of acres of land. Tsars usually chose their advisers from the members of these families. Most nobles, though, had only small amounts of land under their control. They were neither rich nor powerful.

The overwhelming majority of Russians were poor, devoutly religious, hardworking peasants. Most resided in tiny villages, scratching out a living on small plots of land that belonged to a noble or to the government. Although peasants often rebelled against their poverty and blamed the nobles for their troubles, they never seriously challenged the power of the nobles or the tsar.

In the 1800s, though, two new groups emerged in Russia that challenged the country's political and economic system. University students and other educated Russians made up one group, while factory workers made up the second. These groups would lead a revolution in 1917 that would bring an end to tsarist rule in Russia.

Chapter

1 Emergence of Russia: History Before 1598

The Russian Empire began when various kingdoms of Slavs in the areas between the Baltic Sea and the Black Sea united into a single empire in the late 800s. Since the leader of the empire was the prince of Kiev, a city in southwestern Russia overlooking the Dnieper River, it is known as Kievan Russia. At its peak, around 1050, Kievan Russia included over seven million people. It stretched about eight hundred miles north to south and nearly six hundred miles east to west.

An empire built by trade, Kievan Russia controlled the trade routes along the Volga and Dnieper Rivers. These routes connected the Scandinavian empires around the Baltic Sea with the Islamic empires in Turkey and Persia and the Greek Empire based in Byzantium.

The Kievan government protected merchants and their cargo from attacks by bandits, including the nomadic raiders from the east called Tatars, or Tartars. To pay for protecting the trade routes, the prince of Kiev collected a tax, called a tribute, from the prince of each kingdom in the empire.

Goods sold by Russians to Scandinavia, Turkey, Persia, and Greece included grain, furs, honey, and beeswax. Profits from these sales made the princes and merchants of Kievan Russia prosperous. The most valuable items sold by Russians,

though, were humans. People who fell into debt or were captured in feuds among nobles could be enslaved and sold. "The prince of Kiev was famed as a slave dealer,"[1] claims historian R. D. Charques.

Peasant Life in Kievan Russia

Merchants and princes dominated trade with foreign lands, but they were a small part of the population of Kievan Russia. Over 85 percent of the people in the empire were peasants. The grain, animals, honey, and beeswax that peasants sold to merchants or paid in taxes to local princes provided the goods that were sold in foreign lands. Thus, peasants provided the basis of the wealth that made merchants and princes prosperous.

Despite their important role in the empire, most peasants led short, hard, desperate lives. Only one bad harvest separated them from starvation. In *The Chronicle of Novgorod*, a writer from that city in northern Russia describes a famine during the year 1128:

This year it was cruel . . . the people ate lime tree leaves, birch bark;

Russian Women

Just as the rich were considered superior to the poor, so men were considered superior to women in Russia in the 1500s. In "Notes upon Russia," Sigismund von Herberstein commented on the lives of Russian women. This account is quoted in Medieval Russia, *edited by Basil Dmytryshyn.*

"The condition of women is most miserable; for they consider no woman virtuous unless she live shut up at home, and be so closely guarded that she go out nowhere. They give a woman, I say, little credit for modesty, if she be seen by strangers or people out of doors. But shut up at home they do nothing but spin and sew, and have literally no authority or influence in the house. All the domestic work is done by the servants. Whatever is strangled by the hands of a woman, whether it be a fowl, or any other kind of animal, they abominate [condemn] as unclean. The wives, however, of the poorer classes do the household work and cook. But if their husbands and the men-servants happen to be away, and they wish to strangle a fowl, they stand at the door holding the fowl, or whatever other animal it may be, and a knife, and generally beg the men that pass by to kill it. They are very seldom admitted into the churches, and still less frequently to friendly meetings, unless they be very old and free from all suspicion. On certain holidays, however, men allow their wives and daughters, as a special gratification [reward], to meet in very pleasant meadows, where they seat themselves on a sort of wheel of fortune, and are moved alternately up and down, or they fasten a rope somewhere, with a seat to it, in which they sit, and are swung backwards and forwards; or they otherwise make merry with clapping their hands and singing songs, but they have no dances whatever."

pounded wood pulp mixed with husks and straw; and some ate buttercups, moss, horseflesh; and thus many dropping down from hunger, their corpses were in the streets, in the market place, and on the roads, and everywhere. They hired hirelings [workers] to carry the dead out of the town; the serfs could not go out [because the smell was so bad]; woe and misery on all! Fathers and mothers would put their children into boats in gift to merchants or else put them to death; and others dispersed over [moved to] foreign lands. Thus did our country perish on account of our sins.[2]

After Kievan ruler Vladimir (center) converted to Christianity in 988, many Russians incorporated the worship of nature gods into the new religion.

Christianity

Peasants, like the writer from Novgorod, often blamed themselves for disasters they suffered. They believed that famines, as well as floods, disease, and other evils, were punishments from one of the many gods they worshiped. Most Russians, like their Slavic ancestors, believed in a variety of nature gods, such as Stribog the wind god and Perun the god of thunder. They thought that spirits lived in trees, plants, and special places and that if they said a particular prayer or recited a particular saying to these spirits, it might bring good luck to one's family or cure an illness. After 988, when the Kievan ruler Vladimir converted to Christianity, most Russian peasants added Christian beliefs to their religion. Some Christian leaders condemned the combination of Christian and non-Christian beliefs, but they could not stop it. This system of dual belief remained common in Russia into the early 1900s.

While Christianity was a latecoming religion to most Russians, it had a tremendous impact on Russian history. For example, it influenced Russia's relationship with its neighbor to the west, Poland. When Vladimir converted in 988, he adopted a form of Christianity known as Orthodoxy, which was practiced in Byzantium, the capital of the powerful empire to Russia's south. In contrast, Poland, and most of Europe, followed the form of Christianity used in Rome, which became known as Roman Catholicism. Orthodox and Roman Catholic styles of Christianity differed in many details. For example, Orthodox priests can marry, but Roman priests cannot. Partly because of these religious differences, Russia and Poland have had a history of suspicion of each other. These suspicions, along with political and economic conflicts, have led to frequent wars between Russia and Poland.

Christianity also shaped Russia's choice of allies. Russia has had close cultural and political ties with other Orthodox countries, such as Greece and Serbia. These ties still remain strong. In World War I, which began in 1914, and in the Balkan crisis of the 1990s, Russia's support for Serbia shaped its policies.

Finally, Christianity contributed to what may be the most important legacy of Kievan Russia. That was a change in how Russians viewed themselves. In part, Russians' adherence to Orthodox Christianity allowed Russians to begin to develop a sense of identity as a nation, which historian R. D. Charques calls "a unifying sense among the tribes of a common Slav inheritance."[3] People descended from various kingdoms of Slavs began to think of themselves as one people.

The Mongols

Throughout its history Kievan Russia had fought off Tatars invading from the east. In the 1200s came the most terrifying of these invaders: the Mongols.

Beginning in 1206 the Mongols, led by Genghis Khan, moved outward in all directions from their homeland in central Asia. They conquered almost all of Asia and Europe. It became, claims historian Melvin C. Wren, "the largest empire the world has ever known."[4] Though their population never exceeded one million, the Mongols controlled an empire of one hundred million people. Through terror, trade, and tribute they ruled for two centuries. In 1243 one writer, quoted by historian Warren Bartlett Walsh, concluded that the Mongols "were above all men, covetous, hasty, deceitful and merciless. . . . They think that all things are created for themselves alone. . . . Vanquished, they ask no favor; and vanquishing, they show no compassion."[5]

One of the first Russian cities to fall to the Mongols was Ryazan, a city five hundred miles northeast of Kiev. Historians Janet G. Vaillant and John Richards II quote a writer of that time who described what happened in 1237:

The Tatars came to the Cathedral of the Assumption of the Blessed Virgin, and they cut to pieces the Great Princess Agrippina, her daughters-in-law, and other princesses. They burned to death the bishops and the priests and put the torch to the holy

A religious procession in Moscow. Christianity played a vital role in Russian history, particularly because it unified the various peoples within the Russian Empire.

church. And the Tatars cut down many people, including women and children. Still others were drowned in the river. And they killed without exception all monks and priests. And they burned this holy city with all its beauty and wealth, and they captured the relatives of the Riazan [Ryazan] princes, the princes of Kiev and Chernigov. And churches of God were destroyed, and much blood was spilled on the holy altars. And not one man remained alive in the city. All were dead. And this happened for our sins.[6]

Not everyone suffered under the Mongols. After conquering a region, the Mongols wanted only their tribute. They did not require conquered people to change their languages, customs, or religion. As a result, the Russian Orthodox Church remained strong under Mongol rule. In addition, Russians had a chance for success in the military. According to historian Joan Hasler, "Whenever Genghis [Khan] defeated an army he made the men join him and trained them like the others [the Mongols]. Those who were brave and loyal were rewarded with high office."[7]

Advice on Rearing Children

The right of a parent to sell a child into slavery suggests the hard life that children in Russia had in the 1500s. These suggestions to parents are from the Domostroy, *a book of advice on managing a household reprinted in Warren Walsh,* Readings in Russian History. *It was probably written by advisers to Ivan the Terrible. The translation is by Leo Wiener.*

"Punish your son in his youth, and he will give you a quiet old age, and restfulness to your soul. Weaken not beating the boy, for he will not die from your striking him with the rod, but will be in better health; for while you strike his body, you save his soul from death. If you love your son, punish him frequently, that you may rejoice later. Chide [correct] your son in his childhood, and you will be glad in his manhood, and you will boast among evil persons, and your enemies will be envious. Bring up your child with much prohibition, and you will have peace and blessing from him. Do not smile at him, or play with him for though that will diminish your grief while he is a child, it will increase when he is older, and you will cause much bitterness to your soul. Give him no power in his youth, but crush his ribs while he is growing and does not in his wilfulness obey you, lest there be an aggravation and suffering to your soul, a loss to your house, destruction to your property, scorn from your neighbors and ridicule from your enemies, and cost and worriment from the authorities."

The Mongols also revived ancient trade routes connecting Europe and Asia, which had been almost unusable for nearly one thousand years because of fear of robbers. Many Russian merchants grew wealthy under the stability of Mongol rule.

As happened throughout Russia's history, however, the peasants suffered under Mongol rule. Rebuilding after raids and paying tribute absorbed all the wealth they produced. In the judgment of one historian, the peasants "lost all hope of rising above the barest subsistence"[8] under the Mongols.

The Moscow Princes

Over time, though, disputes among rival Mongol leaders loosened the invaders' grip on Russia. So the Mongols appointed Russians to collect tribute. Historian Wren explains how this practice allowed the prince of Moscow to become powerful:

> The prince of Moscow, cringing and servile [slavelike] to his Mongol master, was imperious [dominant] and haughty to the other Russian princes over whom he ruled in the khan's name. He was completely without pity when empowered to lead a Mongol army to punish those of his countrymen who defied or resisted the khan's authority, or his own as the khan's lieutenant. Steadily but shrewdly and almost stealthily the Moscow prince increased his power during those centuries of alien rule until he became by far the most powerful prince in all Russia.[9]

By the 1400s Mongol rule was growing weaker, and the Moscow princes were getting stronger. The stage was set for a new Russian empire.

Expanding Moscow's Empire

In 1462 Ivan III became ruler of Moscow. When he took power, his empire was smaller than today's American state of West Virginia. Though the Mongols still claimed tribute, their weakening power allowed Ivan III to refuse to pay it. The Mongols sent troops to collect tribute, but Ivan III's army was able to hold them off. Finally, in 1480, "Ivan III publicly renounced any allegiance to the Golden Horde,"[10] according to historian Nicholas V. Riasanovsky. Moscow became free from Mongol domination. For this accomplishment, among others, Ivan III is known as Ivan the Great.

Besides throwing off the Mongols, Ivan the Great fought to regain control over lands that were once part of the Kievan Russian Empire. Although he was not an exceptionally brave or great general, he was in charge of a powerful army. His most important conquest was to the north: the region of Novgorod. In 1487 Novgorod was a key trading center on the Lovat River. It controlled territory as far as the Pechora River one thousand miles to the east. Ivan III was a harsh conqueror. Historian Basil Dmytryshyn quotes a later account by Sigismund von Herberstein, ambassador from the Holy Roman Empire in the early 1500s, that the Moscow forces "reduced the inhabitants [of Novgorod] to the most abject [lowly] servitude, and seizing the gold and silver and all the goods of the citizens, carried off more than three hundred waggons full of booty."[11]

By conquering Novgorod, Ivan the Great crushed an early form of democracy in Russian lands. Novgorod had been governed by a city assembly. Ivan ended this practice at once. According to historian

Ivan III, pictured here on horseback surrounded by his subjects, released Russia from the Mongols' grip in 1480.

Henry Moscow, Ivan immediately jailed Novgorod's woman mayor and moved "to Moscow the bell that had summoned Novgorod's city assembly. 'There shall be no veche [assembly] and no bell in our land of Novgorod,' he proclaimed."[12]

Ivan's dislike of popular participation in government reflected the attitudes of most leaders of his time. They did not believe that all people were created equal. Rather, they thought that some people—the wealthy—were from birth morally superior to others—the poor. This attitude about the difference between the wealthy and the poor could be seen in court cases. According to the Roman Empire's ambassador, Herberstein, even in the early sixteenth century "the testimony of one nobleman is worth more than that of a multitude of low condition." He describes a judge who received bribes from both sides in a court case. The judge ruled "in the favor of the one who had made him the largest presents" because "the man in whose favor he had given judgment was rich, and held an

honorable position in life, and therefore more to be believed than the other, who was poor and abject [lowly]."[13]

Restrictions on Peasants

The rise of Ivan the Great and the decline of Mongol power seemed to promise more opportunity for peasants. Without the dangers posed by the Mongols, the lands in the east seemed to offer a place where peasants could find land and create better lives for themselves. According to historian Walsh,

> The subsiding of the Tatar menace . . . [meant that] the borderlands were less subject to recurrent raids. The opening up of new lands and the creation of new estates created a brisk competition for labor while at the same time offering greater chances for personal freedom if the peasant could escape toward the frontiers.[14]

However, the apparent opportunity never developed. If peasants moved away from the lands they worked, the nobles who controlled that land would have no one to work it. To prevent the loss of the nobles' workforce, Ivan the Great issued laws that made moving from one place to another more difficult for peasants. By 1497 peasants could move away from their estates only one day each fall. This was the festival day known as St. George's Day.

The Legacy of Ivan the Great

Ivan the Great died peacefully in 1505. He was sixty-five, an old man for his time. During his reign he had thrown off the Mongols and tripled the size of the Moscow empire. He had become more than just the prince of a small region around Moscow. He was the ruler of a new and growing Russian empire. One sign of this change was that he sometimes called himself tsar. This Russian term for a ruler with unlimited power may have come from the Roman word *caesar*, meaning "emperor." Beginning with his grandson, Ivan IV, and until 1917, Russian rulers would formally be called tsars.

Ivan the Terrible

Ivan the Great's son, Vasily, succeeded him. Vasily continued his father's autocratic rule. When he caught an infection and died in 1533, his three-year-old son was in line to become tsar as Ivan IV. Since he was a child, a group of nobles ran the government for him.

Ivan IV's childhood was marred by conflict. Rival nobles were constantly maneuvering for power. Hence, say historians James P. Duffy and Vincent L. Ricci, "Murders, beatings, and verbal and physical abuse became commonplace in the palace."[15] For special ceremonies the nobles dressed young Ivan IV in lavish robes and honored him in public. The rest of the time, though, the nobles treated Ivan IV more like a servant than royalty. Ivan recalled being cold and hungry and treated with contempt by the nobles who ran the government.

In 1547, when Ivan IV was seventeen years old, he declared himself ready to govern. By this time, due to the years of mistreatment under the nobles, he had developed both a bitter hatred of them and a cruel, violent temper. Because of his cruelty, Ivan IV's nickname, Grozny, is often translated as "Terrible." Ivan the Terrible became one of the most feared tsars of Russian history. Historian Dmytryshyn quotes an ambassador from England, Giles Fletcher, who describes the casualness with which Ivan ordered people executed:

> To show his sovereignty over the lives of his subjects, the late emperor Ivan Vasilevich, in his walks or progresses, if he had misliked the face or person of any man whom he met by the way, or that looked upon him, would command his head to be struck off. Which was presently done, and the head cast before him.[16]

Most of his violence, though, was directed at the nobles who challenged his authority. Much of the land that Ivan the Terrible ruled had been made part of his empire by force. Many nobles in these lands never wanted Moscow to rule them.

To insure that all nobles obeyed him, Ivan the Terrible established his own six-thousand-officer police force, the Oprichniki. "Their purpose," says author Riasanovsky, "was to destroy those whom the tsar considered to be his enemies."[17] The symbol of the Oprichniki was a broom: They were to sweep the land clean of the tsar's enemies. Since they reported directly to the tsar, regular laws and courts did not apply to them. They committed arson, torture, and murder without worrying about punishment. The number of people they killed may have reached into the tens of thousands.

Ivan was an ambitious man who wanted to increase the territory under his control. To the southeast, he added the cities of Kazan and Astrakhan to the empire of Moscow. To the north, his troops

Ivan the Terrible is renowned for his violent temper, which he directed mainly at nobles who challenged his authority.

spent twenty-four years fighting for control of Livonia. They finally had some success, winning control of much of the region. Because of the high cost of these wars, Ivan the Terrible had to keep taxes high. English visitor Giles Fletcher declares that Russian taxes "exceed all just measure."[18] The burden of these taxes fell heavily on the peasants.

The most important expansion under Ivan the Terrible, though, was fairly inexpensive. To the east, Russians pushed beyond the Ural Mountains, battling the nomadic groups living there. Leading the drive was the legendary figure Yermak Timofeyevich. A fearless fighter with a lust for wealth, Yermak was, declares historian Philip Longworth, "a venturer as remarkable as Magellan, a conquistador as fearsome as Cortez."[19] Yermak and two thousand men conquered the city of Sibir in 1580. This city became a steppingstone to the conquest of the entire region east of the Ural Mountains known as Siberia. Waves of Russians moved into Siberia following Yermak's conquests. Some went in search of land, but even more went for the furs. The export of Siberian furs to Europe became a major source of wealth for Russia in the 1600s and 1700s.

Evaluating Ivan the Terrible

Despite Ivan the Terrible's cruelty and his high taxes, many peasants admired him. They were especially sympathetic to his brutal treatment of the nobles. According to historian E. M. Almedingen, "the common folk" argued that the nobility "had oppressed the poor for generations and now they had their deserts."[20] In fact, says

The Russian Character

Giles Fletcher was impressed with both the brutality of Ivan the Terrible and the customs of the Russian people. In this excerpt from his book The Russe Commonwealth, *as quoted by Basil Dmytryshyn, he comments on some of the customs he encountered.*

"The Russian, because that he is used to both these extremities of heat and cold, can bear them both a great deal more patiently than strangers can do. You shall see them sometimes (to season their bodies) come out of their bathstoves all on a froth, and fuming as hot almost as a pig at a spit, and presently to leap into the river stark naked, or to pour cold water all over their bodies, and that in the coldest of all the winter time. The women, to mend the bad hue of their skins, used to paint their faces with white and red colors, so visibly that every man may perceive it. Which is made no matter, because it is common and liked well by their husbands, who make their wives and daughters an ordinary allowance to buy them colors to paint their faces withal, and delight themselves much to see them of foul women to become such fair images. This parches the skin, and helps to deform them when their painting is off."

author Riasanovsky, Ivan's nickname, Grozny, "implied admiration rather than censure [criticism] and referred to his might."[21] Historian Ivar Spector suggests that translating Grozny as awe-inspiring, great, or wonderful would more accurately reflect how Russians used the term. A Russian folk poem composed after Ivan's death demonstrates this respect:

Why bright moon, father moon
Dost thou not shine as of Old?

. . . .

In the coffin lies the Orthodox Tsar,
The Orthodox Tsar, Ivan Vasilievich,
the formidable.[22]

While they may have admired Ivan, peasants did not gain any economic ground under him. In fact, the restrictions on the movement of peasants that began under Ivan the Great became tighter under Ivan the Terrible. According to historian Spector, "beginning in 1581, certain years were designated as 'prohibited,' and the peasant had to remain on a given estate during such a year. It was but a step, then, to make all years 'prohibited,' and the peasant became 'attached' to the soil without freedom to leave."[23]

Over the years more peasants became bound to the land they worked. If the owner sold the land, the peasants went with it, just as the buildings did. Peasants who lived on land owned by nobles were called serfs. Those who lived on lands owned by the government or by the

Ivan the Terrible cradles his dead son. During an argument, Ivan lost his temper and struck his son with an iron staff, killing him.

church became known as state peasants. By the 1680s almost all peasants belonged to either the nobles or the state. Without the freedom to move, peasants had almost no way to escape poverty. They were caught in a system that made prosperity very difficult. Until the 1860s, no significant reform would offer peasants hope for their future. Most Russians would remain poor while a few became wealthy.

Whatever the translation of his nickname, Ivan IV left Russia a powerful legacy. In the long term he firmly established the tradition that the tsar's power was absolute, unchecked by law or the nobles. Anyone who opposed the tsar had to be ready to die. For more than three and a half centuries following Ivan's death, when the tsar was strong, neither the nobles nor the peasants could check any abuses of power. When the tsar was weak, the country was without leadership.

In the short term, Ivan's legacy was equally powerful. In a fit of rage he had killed the only one of his children who showed the ability to govern Russia. According to Russian historian V. O. Kliuchevsky, Ivan

> gave a beating to his pregnant daughter-in-law because when he came into her room he found her too scantily clad. . . . Her husband, Tsarevich Ivan, heir to the throne, stood up for his insulted wife, and his father, in a fit of rage, struck him dead with an unfortunately effective blow of his iron staff. The Tsar almost went out of his mind with grief for his son.[24]

In 1584, after years of poor health, Ivan the Terrible died. His death left the country without a strong ruler. Russia soon plunged into an era of turmoil even worse than under the bloody tyrant.

2 Growth of an Empire: 1598–1725

After Ivan the Terrible's death in 1584, his sickly son Fyodor became tsar. In 1598, Fyodor died without a clear successor, setting off a number of battles over who should be the rightful tsar. This struggle, along with a terrible famine, would combine to become one of the most turbulent eras in Russia's difficult history, a fifteen-year period known as the Time of Troubles.

The Famine

In 1601 an early frost destroyed many crops before they could be harvested. The following year crops were bad again. By the end of 1602 many peasants were on the brink of starvation. "Thousands of dispossessed, desperate men and women wandered about, marauding and killing for the sake of food,"[25] says historian E. M. Almedingen. People tried to survive by eating grass and straw. Reports of cannibalism were widespread.

To make the famine even more deadly, some Russians with money saw a chance to make even more. Authors R. E. F. Smith and David Christian quote one observer: "The devil of greed, allowed by God as a punishment for the whole land, so seized the rich Moscow profiteers that they started to buy up [grain] at a low price and then to resell it to the poor much dearer [at a higher price]."[26]

The tsar during the famine was Boris Godunov, Fyodor's brother-in-law. As the death toll from the famine mounted, Godunov wanted to hand out food that the government held in storage. His efforts, though, were blocked by powerful nobles who opposed his rule. These nobles would support no policy that increased the tsar's popularity, even if Russians continued to starve.

By the end of the famine, over one hundred thousand people had died in Moscow alone. Many died needlessly as a result of the selfishness of politicians and the greed of merchants.

Crisis in Leadership

The nobles who wanted to undermine Godunov's rule did not consider him the rightful tsar. Throughout his reign, various ambitious individuals declared themselves the legitimate ruler of the empire. Most claimed that they were relatives of Fyodor or an earlier tsar, and hence rightful heir. For example, one man said he was Fyodor's son, even though Fyodor's only child was a daughter who had died in infancy.

Several individuals claimed to be Fyodor's half-brother, Dmitri. The real Dmitri had died at the age of nine in 1591 when he reportedly accidentally fell on a knife. Many suspected that Godunov had had Dmitri murdered in order to remove a possible rival to the throne. Just as persistent were rumors claiming that Dmitri was still alive, hidden by loyal supporters. Yet another rumor claimed that he was still alive but that his death had been faked so that Godunov and others would not try to murder him. Many Russians believed that Godunov's supporters had tried to kill Dmitri but that God had saved the boy from death with a miracle. These rumors continued throughout the Time of Troubles.

Battle for the Throne

Despite challenges from various rivals, Godunov reigned from 1598 to 1605. When he died, possibly from poisoning, the battle for the throne became even more heated. Each would-be tsar raised an army to help him seize and hold power. Some had as many as thirty thousand soldiers under their command. Hoping to take advantage of the divisions among Russians and seize control of all or part of the country, Sweden invaded Russia, seizing control of part of Novgorod. Poland also invaded Russia. In 1610 the Polish army attacked and won control of Moscow. With the most powerful city in Russia under its control, Poland prepared to install the son of the Polish king as tsar. The son, like most Poles, was a Roman Catholic.

The threat of a Polish Roman Catholic tsar terrified many Russians. A group of clergy and minor nobles stepped forward to lead resistance against the foreigners. They formed an army of nearly one hundred thousand soldiers and drove the Poles out of Moscow. By September 1612 Moscow was again controlled by Russians.

But the Russians still had no established ruler. Russian leaders, mostly nobles, gathered to select a new tsar. Their choice was sixteen-year-old Michael Romanov, grandnephew of Ivan IV. As quoted by historian Walsh, Michael was described by one person at the time as "kind, mild, gentle, meek and well-intentioned" but

After years of fighting for control of Russia, a group of clergy and nobles emerged victorious and selected Michael Romanov as their new tsar.

that "he had not enough strength of mind to govern the country."[27] This was exactly what the nobles who selected Michael wanted: a ruler too weak to bother them. Michael was so insignificant that at the moment he was chosen tsar, no one knew where he was to notify him.

Despite Michael's seeming insignificance, his selection and reign are notable for three reasons. First, Russia had united to oust a non-Russian, non-Orthodox tsar. Second, Moscow's importance as the center of the Russian government was clearly established. Third, Michael's reign would be the first by a Romanov, making him the founder of a new dynasty. Members of the Romanov family would rule Russia until 1917.

Expanding the Empire

Michael ruled Russia for thirty-two years. His greatest achievements came soon after taking office. In 1617 Russia signed a treaty with Sweden in which it regained most of Novgorod, though Sweden kept land along the Gulf of Finland. A year later Russia signed a treaty with Poland. Poland was allowed to retain control over the city of Smolensk in exchange for freeing Michael's father, Philaret, who was captured during the fighting in 1610.

After Michael died in 1645, his son Alexis became tsar. Like many Russians, Alexis was eager to see Russia resume its conquest of new territory. In particular he wanted to regain control over Ukraine. This region, which included Kiev, had been controlled by non-Russians since the 1200s. Because Poland had ruled the area since 1569, claiming Kiev would mean war with Poland.

In 1648 Alexis saw a convenient way to accomplish his goal when the people in Ukraine rebelled against Polish rule. Most of the rebels were Orthodox Christians who wanted more power to control their own region. Fearing they were too weak to defeat the Roman Catholic Poles on their own, the rebels sought aid from their Orthodox neighbor, Russia. The rebels agreed to make Ukraine part of Russia if the tsar's troops would help them battle the Poles. Russia accepted the rebels' proposal, and the war with Poland began. After several years of fighting and several more years of negotiating, Russia and Poland finally signed an agreement in 1667 that divided Ukraine. Russia won control of Kiev and the surrounding region.

Acquiring part of Ukraine was significant far beyond the simple addition of more land to Russia. It brought a new group under tsarist rule: the Cossacks. Most Cossacks were former peasants who had fled harsh landlords in Russia or Poland and had established communities along the Dnieper or Don Rivers. Famous as fighters, many Cossacks had long provided military service to the rulers of Russia and Poland. For example, Russian tsars had hired Cossack troops to fend off invasions from Tatars in the east. Ivan the Terrible had hired the Cossack leader Yermak and his band of soldiers to explore Siberia. During the Time of Troubles Cossacks had helped both the Polish invaders attacking Moscow and the Russians defending Moscow. After 1667, with the land of the Cossacks part of Russia, they would become even more important in Russian history. Throughout the 1700s and the 1800s Cossacks were feared as the fiercest fighters among the tsar's troops, as well as the most brutal leaders of peasant uprisings.

The Power of the Tsar

In 1613 Russia was weak from years of famine and war. Yet, according to historian Jerome Blum, in some ways the tsar was the most powerful ruler in Europe. In the following excerpt from Lord and Peasant in Russia from the Ninth to the Nineteenth Century, *Blum describes how the entire Russian society was organized to make the tsar powerful.*

"The Time of Troubles was over. With the accession of the first Romanov the long struggle to create a unified and absolute monarchy was brought to a successful conclusion. The rulers of Moscow from Vasilii II through Ivan IV had earned for themselves the highest rank among Europe's royal statemakers of the fifteenth and sixteenth centuries. The rulers of France, Spain, and England successfully established a new kind of monarchy, but none of them had been able to gain as much power for themselves as the Muscovite [Moscow] princes had. The state over which Michael was called to rule was a unique kind of political organization. It was a Service State and the tsar was its absolute ruler. The activities and the obligations of all subjects, from the greatest lord to the meanest peasant, were determined by the state in the pursuit of its own interests and policies. Every subject was bound to certain specific functions that were designed to preserve and to aggrandize [increase] the power and authority of the state. The seigniors [nobles] were bound to service in the army and the bureaucracy, and the peasants were bound to the seigniors to provide them with the means to perform their state service. Whatever privileges or freedoms a subject might enjoy were his only because the state allowed them to him as a perquisite [privilege] of the function he performed in its service."

While Russia was slowly winning control of the land of the Cossacks, it was rapidly winning control of Siberia. Lured by furs, more and more Russians moved farther and farther into Siberia. As Russians explored the region, they found more than furs to interest them: timber, salt, and an assortment of minerals. Among those supplying the labor to build roads and dig mines in Siberia were many prisoners. Criminals and many political opponents of the tsar were exiled to Siberia where they slaved away in work camps. In three decades Russian colonists advanced the border three thousand miles—all the way to the Pacific Ocean. No other country has conquered such a large frontier so quickly.

The Russians were not moving into empty land. Siberia was already inhabited by numerous small groups of people. Many lived by fishing or hunting in the Siberian woodlands. Some, such as the Dolgany in the north, herded reindeer. Others, such as the Buryats who lived near Lake Baikal in southern Siberia, raised sheep. Cattle were herded by many groups, including the Kamchadales, who lived along the Pacific Ocean. When the Russians appeared, many Siberian natives began to supplement their incomes by trading with them.

Russians brought more than trade items to the Siberians. They brought disease germs that the natives had never encountered. As a result of the spread of these diseases, the native population declined sharply. For example, the Yukagirs

A Cossack. The Cossacks, who lived in Ukraine, were famous for their fighting ability and often provided military service to both Russia and Poland.

were hunters who lived near the Lena River. Their population declined from five thousand to fifteen hundred after contact with Russian settlers. Among the Siberians who survived, many married Russians. Consequently, today many Russians have native Siberian ancestors.

Conservatism in Religion

Russia's territorial expansion under Tsar Alexis made the country larger and stronger. However, the most important developments in Alexis's reign concerned two religious battles that subsequently divided Russians from one another and weakened the country.

The first of these battles was waged between Christians and Jews. While Russians tolerated Muslims and most types of Christians except Roman Catholics, many had no tolerance for Jews. Prejudice against Jews, called anti-Semitism, was widespread among Christians in Russia and throughout Europe. In Russia "there were open massacres [of Jews]," records historian W. Bruce Lincoln, "and between 1648 and 1658, almost a quarter-million Jews perished."[28]

The second battle grew out of an effort to reform the Russian Orthodox Church. Russian church services were conducted in a nearly extinct language, Old Church Slavonic. Hence, virtually no Russian peasants understood what was said during the service. Understanding the words, though, was not considered necessary. Peasants viewed the words read during services the same way they viewed magic spells. Each word had to be said correctly, or the service could have no effect. Since it was the saying of the words and not their meaning that was important, some churches would have clergy reading different parts of the service at the same time in order to shorten the service.

By the mid-1600s, though, scholars realized that when the Russian church service had been translated into Old Church Slavonic from Greek centuries earlier, some of the words had been translated incorrectly. Russian clergy had been reading the church service with errors in it for generations. Further, Russians followed many customs that differed slightly from those of other Orthodox countries. For example, Russians made the sign of the cross—a gesture made with the hand in front of the body—differently than did other Christians. The Russians used two fingers rather than three in the hand making the gesture.

Eastward Ho!

Russian expansion into Siberia was dangerous and violent. Excerpted here is part of a report from one explorer, Ivan Uvarov, who writes about his unsuccessful search for a missing government official in Siberia in 1652. The document was reprinted in Vernadsky's A Source Book for Russian History.

"While we encamped the Giliak [a group of Siberian natives] men attacked us from many boats, and God helped us to sink one boat and kill the men in the boat, some forty of them; and from there we, the sovereign's slaves, went by sea, rowing, and we rowed out of the bay into the sea, and we, the sovereign's slaves, were tossed amidst the ice on the sea, and we were tossed amidst the ice for ten days and were carried ashore at an uninhabited place, and here the ice pushed us, the sovereign's slaves, against the shore—. The boat was crushed and sank, and we, the sovereign's slaves, managed to get only our bodies and souls ashore; the bread, the lead, and the powder sank into the sea, and all the clothing sank into the sea, and we were left without anything. From there we, the sovereign's slaves, went on foot along the sea, and for five days, we, the sovereign's slaves, walked on foot along the sea, and we lived on berries and herbs, and on the shore we found slaughtered elks, sea animals, seals, and walruses, and with these we defiled [made unclean] our souls, eating them because of our need. . . .

We Ivashko [Ivan] and my companions, here on the Tugir [Tugur] River, are naked and barefoot, and hungry and cold, and perishing utterly from privation [lack of food and clothing], freezing to death from cold, because we have not axes."

In 1652 Alexis appointed Nikon as the leader of the Russian Orthodox Church. Nikon, with the tsar's support, proposed reforms to correct the errors in translation and to make Russian customs conform with those in other Orthodox countries. The reaction to Nikon's reforms was quick and intense. Across the country people exploded in angry defiance. To Archpriest Avvakum, the leading opponent of the reforms, Nikon and the reformers were "filthy dogs, Latins [Roman Catholics] and Jews,"[29] as quoted by George Vernadsky. He attacked them for suggesting any changes in tradition:

> Oh you dogs! What do you have against the olden ways? Impious ones, thieves, sons of whores. . . . If you curse us for [maintaining] the holy olden ways: then also should you curse your fathers and mothers, who died in our faith.[30]

Faced with such widespread opposition over such small changes, Nikon could have backed down. He did not. Haughty, rigid, and convinced that he was right, Nikon pushed ahead. Like the tsar, Nikon believed that the Russian people should follow his orders without question.

After Nikon left office in 1666, the battle worsened. In 1667 the church began excommunicating, or removing from membership in the church, opponents of reform. Many were exiled to Siberia, imprisoned, or killed. Avvakum, for example, was sent to various prison camps for several years. He was finally executed in 1682. Despite persecution, many Russians refused to accept Nikon's changes. Opponents of the reforms became known as Old Believers. Over the next decades as many as twenty thousand Old Believers,

When the patriarch Nikon reformed parts of the Russian church service, he caused an uproar among Russians that divided the Russian Orthodox Church.

believing that the reforms marked the coming of the end of the world, committed suicide. Others lived on, often forming their own tiny communities in remote regions of Siberia where they could worship as they wished.

Despite the fervent opposition of the Old Believers, the reforms were instituted. The split between the mainstream of the church and the Old Believers was never healed. By 1917 Old Believers probably constituted between 10 and 20 percent of the Russian population. Consequently, the Russian Orthodox Church never regained the unity or power it had before Nikon. The role of the church in uniting the population, a role it had played since the days of Kievan Russia and through the Time of Troubles, was over.

How Many Fingers?

Avvakum, the leader of Nikon's opponents, wrote his autobiography while in exile between 1672 and 1676. This excerpt is from the portion of the book reprinted in Vernadsky's A Source Book for Russian History. *Avvakum describes a meeting with religious leaders who supported Nikon's reforms.*

"I spoke of many things in Holy Scripture with the patriarchs. God open my sinful mouth and Christ put them to shame. The last word they spoke to me was this: 'Why,' said they, 'do you remain stubborn? All our Christian lands, the Serbs and Albanians and Wallachians and Romans and Poles, all cross themselves with three fingers; you alone remain obstinate and cross yourself with [two] fingers; it is not seemly [proper].' And I answered them for Christ this way: '. . . Before the time of Nikon, the apostate [a person who leaves a religion], in our Russia under our pious princes and tsars the Orthodox faith was pure and undefiled, and the church was free from turmoil. Nikon the wolf, together with the Devil, ordained that men should cross themselves with three fingers, but our first shepherds made the sign of the cross and blessed men with [two] fingers, according to the tradition of our holy fathers. . . .'

[To his supporters, Avvakum said:] God will bless you: suffer tortures for the way you place your fingers, do not reason too much! And I am ready to die with you for this and for Christ. Even if I am a foolish man and without learning, yet this I know, that all the traditions of the church, handed down to us by the holy fathers, are holy and incorrupt. I will maintain them even unto death, as I received them. I will not alter the eternal rules that were laid down before our time; may they remain so unto ages of ages."

The battle over Nikon's reforms demonstrated how the peasants viewed change: Peasants were fiercely conservative, and any change, no matter how small, might be met with resistance to the death. Russia's leaders were fiercely elitist: They thought that peasants had no right to question their decisions on even the smallest matters. Russia was caught between an unmovable peasantry and unbending rulers.

After Alexis died in 1676, his fourteen-year-old son, Fyodor III, took his place. Never healthy, Fyodor III died six years later. In 1682 two other sons of Alexis became co-tsars. Since they were both still children, other relatives ruled on their behalf. One of the brothers died before becoming old enough to rule independently. The other brother was to become the most influential tsar in Russian history: Peter the Great.

The Childhood of Peter the Great

As a child Peter had a fascination with western Europe. As a teen he spent much of his time in the German Suburb, an area in Moscow where many Europeans lived. He became friends with people from places such as Germany, the Netherlands, England, and Scotland. From these encounters he came to the conclusion that the western Europeans knew far more about mathematics, science, and technology than did the Russians. From his friends he learned geometry and algebra and how to apply this knowledge to practical military concerns, such as aiming artillery accurately and building strong fortifications. This continued fascination with western Europe would be a driving force in his reign.

As Peter reached adulthood, he became a giant for his time—six feet, seven inches tall, maybe taller. But, says historian Robert Massie, "his most extraordinary quality, even more remarkable than his height, was his titanic energy. He could not sit still or stay long in the same place."[31] His energy also propelled his incessant curiosity about every form of practical knowledge. During his life Peter took great pride in learning dozens of trades, from carpentry to dentistry.

Peter's Reforms

In 1694, at the age of twenty-two, Peter became the effective ruler of Russia. He believed that Russia would never be a powerful empire until it caught up with Europe in the area of technology. In particular, the Russian military needed better education and technology to be as strong as the militaries of several smaller countries. Peter believed that Russia must copy the ways of England, France, and the rest of western Europe. It must westernize in order to strengthen its military.

Peter made tremendous efforts to accomplish this goal. He hired foreign technicians to teach Russians how to build better ships and construct stronger fortresses. He set up schools to teach mathematics and engineering that soldiers needed to know to aim cannons accurately and to construct fortresses soundly. He started Russia's first newspaper so that Russians, like Europeans, could read about current events. He abandoned the traditional Russian calendar, which dated events from the creation of the world. In its place he adopted the calendar used in western Europe, which dated events from the birth of Jesus. He opened positions in government to the talented sons of common families instead of just the sons of nobles. He started the Academy of Sciences to promote research and learning. He even ordered people to call him emperor rather than tsar because he believed that emperor sounded more western.

Peter even wanted to change how Russians looked. In 1698, according to Massie, Peter met with several nobles, and "after passing among them and exchanging embraces, Peter suddenly produced a long, sharp barber's razor and with his own hands began shaving off their beards."[32]

Peter soon issued a decree, says Massie, that "all Russians, except the clergy and the peasants were ordered to shave."[33] This was eventually modified so that anyone could wear a beard if he paid a tax on it.

Peter's decrees created an uproar. To Russians beards were more than just a style. They had deep religious significance. According to historian Henri Troyat, a church council had decreed in 1551 that "there is no heretical [antichurch] custom more to be condemned than that of shaving the beard. . . . To shave one's beard in order to be pleasing to men, is to become the enemy of God who created us in his image."[34]

In a country where change was stubbornly opposed, Peter's efforts drew intense, widespread opposition. Russia was still the same harshly conservative country that had bitterly opposed Nikon's comparatively minor reforms during the reign of Peter's father.

Opposing Peter was dangerous because of his violent temper and a willingness to inflict cruel tortures on those he disliked. Biographer Alex de Jonge quotes one female victim of Peter's, who noted, "On days that his Majesty [Peter] and Prince Romondanovsky [the head of Peter's police force] drink blood they are merry, and when they do not their bread seems tasteless."[35] Even Peter's own son did not escape severe punishment. Upon learning that his son and heir did not agree with many of his reforms and planned to undo them when he became tsar, Peter ordered his son jailed. The young man died while being tortured.

Peter viewed torture as necessary to guaranteeing honesty. Hence, both sides in a dispute might be tortured to be sure

Peter the Great, enamored of western European style, ordered Russian nobles to shave their beards. Russians saw this as heresy and vehemently opposed Peter's decree.

that each was telling the truth. According to author de Jonge, he once said that he "did not want an unclean conscience before God, so would never rely upon a denunciation [accusation] that had not been thoroughly tested by torture."[36]

Peter's Military Expansion

Peter's efforts to strengthen the military by copying western Europe were at least partly successful. Russia's military did become larger and stronger under Peter the Great. The Russian military grew to two hundred thousand soldiers and seventy-five thousand sailors. In addition, the tsar

The Influence of Peter the Great

Peter the Great has long been revered—and hated—by Russians more than most other tsars. In the mid-1800s one Russian historian, Mikhail P. Pogodin, surveyed Peter the Great's impact on Russian life. The excerpt is quoted from Nicholas Riasanovsky's A History of Russia.

"We wake up. What day is it today? January 1, 1841—Peter the Great ordered us to count years from the birth of Christ: Peter the Great ordered us to count the months from January.

It is time to dress—our clothing is made according to the fashion established by Peter the First, our uniform according to his model. The cloth is woven in a factory which he created; the wool is shorn from the sheep which he started to raise.

A book strikes our eyes—Peter the Great introduced this script and himself cut out the letters. You begin to read it—this language became a written language, a literary language, at the time of Peter the First, superseding the earlier church language.

Newspapers are brought in—Peter the Great introduced them.

You must buy different things—they all, from the silk neckerchief to the sole of your shoe, will remind you of Peter the Great; some were ordered by him, others were brought into use or improved by him, carried on his ships, into his harbors, on his canals, on his roads.

At dinner, all the courses, from salted herring, through potatoes which he ordered grown, to wine made from grapes which he began to cultivate, will speak to you of Peter the Great."

Peter the Great used western European culture as a model for the numerous changes he implemented in Russia.

could call upon one hundred thousand Cossacks who were pledged to fight for him. Peter hoped that these large forces would enable Russia to control ports on both the Black Sea to the south and the Baltic Sea to the northwest in order to make trade with Europe easier. The existing seaports in the western Russian Empire were in the far north on the White Sea, and ice made these ports unusable during the winter.

In the south Turkey controlled the major port on the Black Sea, Azov. Russian troops attacked Azov in 1695, but they failed to seize it. The following year they attacked again. This time the Russians were successful, but they spent the next four years fighting off Turkish attacks. Russians held Azov until 1711, when the Turks attacked again and regained control of the port.

Peter and the Russians were more successful in getting an outlet to sea in the northwest, where Sweden controlled the land along the Baltic Sea. The conflict between Russia and Sweden, known as the Great Northern War, lasted from 1700 to 1721. Fighting extended throughout western Russia and Ukraine. The first year of the war went badly for Russia. In November 1700 at the Battle of Narva, a Swedish fort on the Baltic Sea, Swedish forces killed or captured ten thousand Russian troops. After the defeat Peter rebuilt his army and improved its training. In 1709, with Peter leading the soldiers into battle, the Russians defeated the Swedes at Poltava, a city southeast of Kiev. The Russian victory at Poltava proved to be a turning point in the war. Fighting lasted until 1721, when Russia and Sweden finally signed a peace treaty. Russia won control

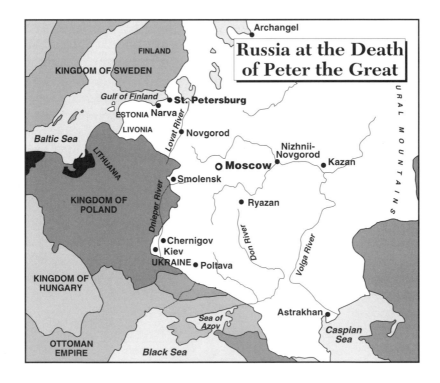

of parts of Livonia and Estonia, two regions on the Baltic Sea.

In 1703, long before the end of that war, though, Russia had seized a strip of land along the Baltic Sea coast where the Neva River runs into the sea. On this marshy land Peter decided to build a grand new city: St. Petersburg. To make his dream real, Peter issued orders requiring thousands of laborers to come to the city to construct buildings, roads, and canals. When he had trouble getting stonemasons to come, he banned the construction of stone buildings in Russia. Masons who wanted work headed to St. Petersburg.

They probably went reluctantly. According to Massie, the human cost of building the city was immense:

> The hardships were frightful. Workers lived on damp ground in rough, crowded, filthy huts. Scurvy, dysentery, malaria and other diseases scythed them down in droves [killed them in large numbers]. Wages were not paid regularly and desertion was chronic. The actual number who died building the city will never be known; in Peter's day, it was estimated at 100,000. Later figures are much lower; perhaps 25,000 or 30,000, but no one disputes the grim saying that St. Petersburg was "a city built on bones."[37]

Yet the power of the tsar was as strong as his will. With an entire country at his disposal, his city was built. As Peter had hoped, St. Petersburg became a major port for trade between Russia and Europe. In addition, for the following two centuries, it served as the capital of Russia.

Peter's Impact on Russia

Peter's relentless drive to modernize Russia made him many enemies among those who loved Russia's traditions. His willingness to attack any problem also brought his death. On January 28, 1725, Peter dove into the water to rescue sailors who were drowning. The plunge into the icy water apparently contributed to his catching an illness that killed him. For a man so committed to action, it was a fitting end to life.

The cost of Peter's reforms was more than emotional and religious. His endless military adventures required money. In 1680, before Peter's policies took effect, the Russian government took in 1.4 million rubles; by 1701 the amount had reached 3 million; and by 1724 Peter's government collected 8.5 million rubles. Military expenditures accounted for as much as 80 percent of the government budget. To raise this money, says Spector, "Peter resorted to innumerable taxes on land, wearing apparel, implements, food, birth, and marriage, most of which weighed heavily upon the peasants."[38] By the time Peter died in 1725, the tax burden was still crushing the peasants. Some of his projects— schools, ships, canals—could have laid the groundwork for economic growth. However, for all of his desire to make Russia into a powerful state, his expensive wars kept it mired in poverty.

3 The Reign of Catherine the Great: 1762–1796

For almost forty years after the death of Peter the Great, Russia suffered under a succession of weak tsars. In 1762 Catherine II, became tsar after her husband, Tsar Peter II, was murdered. Whether Catherine wanted her husband killed is not clear, but she supported the plot to remove him from power.

Catherine was extravagant from the start of her reign. Hoping to impress her subjects, she organized a stunning coronation ceremony. The crown made for her required a pound of gold and twenty pounds of silver. The mantle used four thousand ermine skins. Silver coins—enough to fill over one hundred kegs—were thrown into the crowds. After the ceremony the government held a tremendous feast for the public.

These efforts contributed to her popularity, with many Russians lovingly referring to her as Little Mother. Historian Henri Troyat describes how crowds of citizens would surround Catherine as she walked to church. Once, when the police pulled out their whips to drive the people off, Catherine "stretched out her arms to protect her people. This symbolic gesture brought forth sobs of gratitude from the crowd. . . . [Such stories] retold a thousand times, exaggerated, embroidered, became a legend to the glory of the Little Mother."[39]

Catherine in Power

The coronation was just the beginning of Catherine's lavish spending. She collected the finest art, wore the most expensive clothes, and gave elaborate parties. In addition, though she never remarried, she befriended one man after another. Her openness about these relationships shocked many Russians. When she tired of a man, she would send him off with lavish gifts—vast sums of money, precious gems, and thousands of serfs. Still, says historian Virginia Cowles, Catherine was a serious ruler:

> Despite these distractions Catherine flung herself into the business of ruling with an intensity that amazed even those acquainted with her boundless energy. She rose at six in the morning, rubbed her face with ice, and drank five cups of black coffee.[40]

Catherine often worked fifteen hours a day—reading reports, listening to advisers, preparing decrees. She wanted to know everything, investigate everything, and reform everything. She wanted to dominate Russia just as Peter the Great had done.

Catherine's foreign policy was also modeled on Peter's. She wanted the empire to grow. To the west, Catherine re-

The coronation of Catherine II. During the extravagant event, the public received silver coins and was treated to a lavish feast.

sumed Russia's long-standing battle with Poland. Between 1772 and 1795 Russia joined with Austria and Prussia—two other rivals of Poland—to completely divide up the country. Poland would not regain its independence for over a century. Russia gained control of much of Ukraine and Lithuania. To the north Russia seized another small portion of land along the Baltic Sea from Sweden in 1787 and 1788. In the south Russia battled Turkey for control of the fertile region along the north coast of the Black Sea. In wars between 1768 and 1774, and from 1787 to 1791, Russia captured these lands. In addition, in 1783 Russia annexed Crimea.

The various conquests under Catherine added about 7 million people, or 20 percent of the total population. Few of these people were ethnically Russians. For example, most of the people living on the lands captured from Poland were Ukrainians, Lithuanians, Poles, or Jews. Some of Russia's new lands, those in the east and the south, were only lightly populated. To develop these regions, Catherine welcomed European immigrants to move into them. By 1798 almost 40,000 Germans had settled along the southern portion of the Volga River. A century later the German population of Russia was almost 1.8 million.

Besides sharing Peter's energy and his expansionist policies, Catherine shared his fascination with ideas from western Europe. But while Peter focused on science and technology, Catherine was intrigued more by philosophy and literature. She was an avid reader of French authors such as Voltaire and Diderot. These two writers were among the leaders of a movement in the late 1700s called the Enlightenment. They emphasized the value of experimentation and reason in learning. This was a dramatic shift from the pre-Enlightenment emphasis on tradition and faith.

Catherine demonstrated her interest in western European ideas in various ways. She collected European art, built English-style parks, and made French a popular language among the nobles. Partly because of western European influences, Catherine established schools for girls, started orphanages, and published a literary journal.

Catherine, more so than any tsar before her, was seriously concerned about the effect of poverty on the peasants. She was the first tsar to encourage her advisers to consider ways to improve peasant life.

Helping the Poor

Peasants loved Catherine the Great more than they did most tsars. To win their hearts, Catherine often used her great power to help individuals. This account from a man who served in her court is from Vincent Cronin's Catherine, Empress of All the Russias.

"One day, early in the morning, [Catherine] saw an old woman in the square opposite the palace, trying to catch a hen; the old woman was running after it, and was worn out by her lack of success. 'Give orders that the poor creature should be helped, and find out what this means,' she said to her footman. Inquiries were made, and it was reported that the old woman's grandson was the kitchen-boy to the Court, and that the hen was State property which was being stolen. 'Make it a rule for ever,' said Catherine, 'that the old woman should be

given a hen every day; only, not a live one, but a dead one. In this way we shall deter [stop] the young man from crime, and relieve his grandmother from her efforts and help her in her poverty.' So from then on the old woman received a chicken as her right."

Catherine's sympathy and generosity toward the public earned her the nickname "Little Mother."

The interior of a peasant home. Because Catherine's humanitarian efforts were funded by tax increases, life became even more difficult for many peasants.

For example, Catherine hoped to improve the poor health of peasants. She was appalled by the high rate of death among infants and by how much that weakened the country. She explained:

> Go to a village, ask a peasant how many children he has. He will reply— it is not uncommon—ten, twelve and even often up to twenty. How many does he have who are still living? He will answer one, two, four. . . . We must reduce the mortality [death] rate, consult doctors, improve the care of young children. . . . They run naked on the snow and ice. The one who survives is vigorous, but nineteen die, and what a loss to the state.[41]

Catherine's advice to "consult doctors" was generally ignored by peasants. When giving birth, some women preferred to be alone. An old folk belief was that the fewer people who knew about the birth, the easier it would be. Other women preferred to have a midwife with them. Besides helping deliver the baby, midwives knew the tradi-tional sayings peasants thought would protect a baby from evil.

Economic Change Under Catherine

Catherine may have wanted to reform and improve peasant life. During her reign, however, life got worse for many peasants. Catherine's pursuits—conquering new lands, living extravagantly, and starting new projects—were expensive. Hence, Catherine needed all the taxes she could get. To raise more money, she increased taxes on the nobles. The nobles, in turn, taxed the peasants in the villages they controlled. The entire village was responsible for payment of the taxes. Nobles collected some taxes in money or in goods, and some in labor. The *obrok* was a tax paid in money or goods. According to Walsh, the *obrok* increased sharply under Catherine: "During the 1760's, the *obrok* was usually between one and two rubles per male.

The Peasant Diet

An old Russian saying was that a meal without bread was not a meal. For most Russian peasants rye bread was the main food in every meal. Historians R. E. F. Smith and David Christian, in their book Bread and Salt: A Social and Economic History of Food and Drink in Russia, *provide a more detailed look at what peasants ate.*

"The peasant diets had remained essentially unchanged over many centuries. By the nineteenth century it is possible to describe this dietary regime in some detail. The provincial surveys undertaken by the Army General Staff in the 1860s depict a diet overwhelmingly dominated by grain. Cabbages, particularly when pickled in salt, were important, but less so than grain, and other vegetables—onions, beetroot, cucumber, peas and radishes, in particular—were common. Potatoes were a recent, but increasingly important supplement, often supplanting porridges and gruels—by 1907 an English traveller could describe potatoes as one of the four main elements of the Russian peasant diet. Milk and dairy products were important, but not eaten in large quantities; milk, sour cream and cottage cheese were used mainly as seasonings in soups or gruel or they were used for children or the sick. Meat was a rare luxury, often eaten only on feast days. Animal fat was used as a seasoning for soups or gruel (*kasha*) on meat days, but 'fast oils' (*postnye masla*) made from vegetable products—hemp-, flax- or millet-seeds—were used on fast days [days when religious customs prohibited eating meat]. Fish was also rare and usually eaten salted or dried, except by those who lived near large rivers. Fruit or berries were collected, but as much for sale as for consumption by those gathering them. This was also true of game and honey, and often of fish as well, and even of much livestock produce. Mushrooms were perhaps the most important of gathered foods, and, like berries, they were often preserved. Honey, the traditional sweetener, and an important preservative, was slowly being ousted by sugar in many areas, but salt remained the most important of all preservatives. Potatoes, sugar, and tea were probably the most important additions to the dietary regime during the nineteenth century."

The amount was steadily increased: two to three rubles in the 1770's; four in the 1780's, five in the 1790's."[42]

The *barschina* was a tax paid with labor. Typically, the *barschina* was three days a week. This supposedly meant that a peasant then had three days a week to work for himself and Sundays for worship. During Catherine's reign, nobles began to make peasants work more than three days a week.

Catherine criticized nobles who overworked their serfs. Yet she could not stop it. While she had absolute power in theory, in practice she relied on the nobles to carry out her orders. Just as she could not stop them from working their serfs harder than custom permitted, she could not stop another practice, the selling of serfs separately from the land they worked and lived on. Serfs had always been tied to the land. While this tie limited their freedom, it also prevented nobles from splitting up serf families by selling away a member. In the late 1700s, though, nobles began selling serfs separately from the land. Dmytryshyn quotes a typical newspaper advertisement of the time: "An officer has for sale a 16 year old girl, formerly belonging to a poor house, who knows how to knit, sew, iron, starch, and dress a lady; she has a nice figure and pretty face."[43] Serfs were being treated more and more like livestock. They could be bought and sold according to the owner's wish. Catherine tried to ban the practice of selling serfs, but her ban was ignored.

Peasants reacted to their worsening plight in various ways. Thousands simply broke the law tying them to the land and fled. They often settled in parts of Ukraine or Siberia that still were sparsely populated. In these regions government control was weak, and the likelihood of recapture less.

Peasants resented the increase in taxes and the hardships placed on them. They began to revolt against the nobles. Most revolts were small, with a mob of a few dozen peasants attacking the local steward hired by the noble to administer the noble's land in a village. Some revolts, though, included thousands of peasants. Whatever the size, the revolts were crushed, and the leaders executed or exiled.

Yet these actions by peasants did not address the fundamental problems facing Russia. The revolts were expressions of anger at a particular noble or steward rather than part of a planned movement to change Russian society. In the era of the American Revolution and the French Revolution, a few Russians hoped their country would have a similar upheaval. These hopes were fueled by rumors that Catherine, inspired by the thoughts of Voltaire and others, would end serfdom. She never considered the idea seriously. When the hoped-for freedom did not come, frustration added to the general resentment. Living in poverty, with virtually no legal protection from greedy landlords and little chance to move away, peasants could only submit—or rebel. By 1773 Russia seemed ripe for widespread revolution by the peasants.

Pugachov's Uprising

One of the peasant revolts that began in the 1770s was led by an imposter who claimed to be Catherine's husband, Peter. Since Peter's assassination in 1762, six other men had claimed to be the rightful tsar. Each had a story of how he had miraculously escaped death. Catherine crushed each quickly.

This seventh man, though, was different. Named Yemelyan Pugachov, he was a Cossack who grew up along the Don River in southern Russia. In September 1773 he had a mere eighty followers. But angry peasants, ready to kill and to die to protest their brutal living conditions, quickly flocked to him. Some of Pugachov's supporters were Old Believers, still upset by Nikon's reforms in the Russian Orthodox Church more than a century earlier. They believed Pugachov would restore traditional practices. Many were non-Russians. According to Henry Moscow, this group included the "Bashkirs, Kalmucks, Kirghiz, Tatars, and Finns who had been absorbed by Russia's expansion."[44] Many of them had never accepted rule from Moscow. Within months Pugachov had thirty thousand armed men supporting his rebellion.

Pugachov's troops were scattered, poorly organized, and undisciplined. They moved from village to village, burning buildings, raping women, and murdering people as they went. Peasants sometimes cheered Pugachov's brutal revenge on equally brutal landlords even as they feared for their own safety. The destruction was awful. Not since the invasions by the Mongols had such devastation wracked Russia.

Catherine sent her troops to crush the rebellion. She wanted it stopped before it threatened her government. Battles raged across southern Russia. The government and the rebels fought for control of cities and rural areas.

Slowly the government's superior strength began to win out. In the fall of 1774 some of Pugachov's associates began fearing defeat. They betrayed him in hopes that the government would treat them less harshly. Pugachov was captured and taken to Moscow. Troyat quotes from a letter to Voltaire, in which Catherine wrote that Pugachov

> has lived like a scoundrel and will die like a coward. . . . He cannot read or write, but he is a bold and determined man. . . . He hopes for pardon because of his courage. If it were only I whom he had offended, his reasoning would be correct and I should pardon him;

Two Russian peasants plow the land. Peasants were tied to the land as serfs; they could be bought or sold by the nobles who controlled the land.

The Foolish German

Russian landlords often hired someone to run each of their estates. This person, called a steward, was often disliked by the peasants even more than was the landlord. The following folktale tells how the peasants got revenge on one steward. It is from a collection of stories entitled Russian Fairy Tales, *compiled by Aleksandr Afanas'ev and translated by Norbert Guterman.*

"On a certain big estate there was a German steward who did not observe the holidays of the Russian folk and forced the peasants to work all the time. One day the village elder came to him and said: 'Tomorrow we have a holiday; work is forbidden.' 'What holiday have you thought up now?' 'St. Nicholas' day, little father.' 'And who is he? Show him to me.' The elder brought him an icon. 'Oh, that is just a wooden board,' said the German. 'It can't do anything to me; I shall work, and so will you.' So the peasants decided to play a trick on the German. Again the elder came to see him, saying: 'Little father, tomorrow we have a holiday.' 'What holiday?' 'St. Hornet's day.' 'Who is he? Show him to me.' The elder brought him to a hollow tree, in which the hornets had a nest. 'There he is,' he said to the steward. The German began to peep in through the cracks and heard the hornets humming and humming. 'How he sings!' said the German. 'He must have drunk some vodka! Well, I am not afraid of him, and will order you to work in any case.' As the German spoke, the hornets flew out and fell to stinging him. 'Ai, ai!' he cried at the top of his lungs. 'I swear I won't order you to work, and I won't work myself—I'll even let the peasants take a whole week's holiday!'"

but this is a case involving the Empire, which has its laws.[45]

Pugachov was sentenced to death. Catherine, in a show of mercy, reversed his sentence: Instead of being quartered and then beheaded, he was beheaded first. Says historian Michael T. Florinsky, "On January 11, 1775, he was executed in Moscow, his head was exhibited on a pole, and in four suburbs of the capital parts of his dismembered body were publicly broken on a wheel and then burned."[46]

The death of Pugachov did not end the government's efforts to crush the uprising. According to Troyat, "Every village had its scaffold raised in the public square. There were hangings, beatings, and deportations. . . . It was expressly forbidden to pronounce the name of 'the fearful rebel' Pugachev."[47]

The violent repression worked. For the final twenty-one years of Catherine's reign, until her death in 1796, only about one rebellion a year occurred.

4 Russia's Resistance to Change: 1796–1856

Catherine the Great's death in 1796 signaled the end of an era of reform. For the next sixty years Russia's leaders would remain dedicated to maintaining traditions rather than confronting the problems that kept the country poor. Despite the conservatism of the tsars and most nobles, though, during this era the foundations of reform were laid.

Alexander I

Catherine died when a blood vessel in her brain burst, leaving her son Paul as tsar. After five years he was killed during a coup led by a group of nobles and supported by his son, Alexander. Handsome, well educated, and charming, Alexander I was only twenty-three years old when he became tsar. Though sympathetic to the suffering peasants, Alexander would upset no Russian tradition. He had no use for the revolutionary ideals spreading through Europe and the United States. The belief that a government's authority came from the consent of the governed was absurd to him. Walsh quotes one of Alexander's friends, who expressed the tsar's sentiments when he said, "Our tsars are not representatives of the peoples, but representatives of Him [God] who rules empires."[48]

War with the French

Alexander I's interest, as was Catherine's and Peter's before him, was in foreign affairs. According to Charques, "he saw himself constantly as military savior of his country and indeed of Europe."[49] In his case, Alexander may have been correct. France was ruled by Napoleon Bonaparte. Backed by a powerful army, Napoleon hoped to rule Europe. Alexander I be-

Tsar Alexander I believed he was appointed by God to rule over the people, not to represent their interests.

Price of Glory

In 1839 the marquis de Custine, a French aristocrat, visited Russia. Seeing St. Petersburg made him reflect on the challenges that Russia faced. This excerpt is from a translation by Phyllis Penn Kohler of his book Journey for Our Time.

"Today you will hear, in Paris or in Russia, any number of Russians become ecstatic over the miraculous effects of the word of the Emperor; and, while they are priding themselves on the results, not one will be moved to pity by the means employed. The word of the Czar has the power to create, they say. Yes, it brings stones to life, but in doing so it kills men. Despite this small reservation, all Russians are proud of the ability to say to us: 'You see, in your country one deliberates three years over the means of rebuilding a theater, whereas our Emperor builds the biggest palace in the world in one year.' This childish triumph does not seem to them too dearly paid for by the death of some paltry thousands of workers sacrificed to this regal impatience, to this imperial fantasy, which becomes, to use a fashionable plural, one of the national glories. As for me, however, being French, I see in this only inhuman pedantry [concern for irrelevant knowledge]. But from one end of this vast Empire to the other, not a single protest is raised against these orgies of absolute sovereignty. . . . It can be said of the Russians, great and small—they are intoxicated with slavery."

lieved it his duty to stop him. As he wrote to his sister, "There isn't room enough in Europe for us both; sooner or later one of us will have to go."[50]

The long-anticipated war between France and Russia began in June 1812. After moving through eastern Europe, Napoleon and 420,000 soldiers invaded Russia. Included in this number were many troops from the regions Napoleon had already seized: Italians, Poles, Swiss, Dutch, Germans, Austrians, Prussians. Within months he added another 150,000. The world had never seen such a powerful army.

The French army headed straight for Moscow. The Russians, no match for the experienced, well-equipped French army, tried only to slow the advance. Believing that a major battle with the French would be a disaster, Alexander and several of his military officers concluded that retreat was the best strategy. According to Florinsky:

The Russian army . . . was much smaller, actually less than 200,000. This being the case, there was little choice for the Russians but to retreat. Vilna fell to the enemy four days after

Napoleon Bonaparte invaded Russia in 1812. Russia's troops were no match for Napoleon's enormous army, and he advanced steadily toward Moscow.

run assaults slowed the French advance, but only a bit. A more important factor that undermined the French advance was that in order to guard their supply lines and to control the land they had captured, the French had to leave troops behind.

By early September Napoleon and his troops were just seventy miles southwest of Moscow. Napoleon had 130,000 troops, still slightly more than the Russians. There, on September 7, the French attacked the village of Borodino. The battle for Borodino would later be recalled by Napoleon, and quoted by biographer Felix Markham, as "the most terrible of all my battles. . . . The French showed themselves worthy of victory, and the Russians worthy of being invincible."[52] On that day thirty thousand French soldiers and fifty thousand Russian soldiers were killed or wounded. Despite heroic efforts, the Russians finally retreated. The French triumphed. They prepared to invade Moscow.

The Russians faced a difficult choice. Should they defend Moscow or retreat even farther east? Losing Moscow seemed unthinkable. Defending it, though, seemed impossible. Russian field marshal Kutuzov finally decided that the country could exist without Moscow, but not without an army. According to historian Eugene Tarle, as long as the army existed, Kutuzov pointed out, Napoleon could not win: "Napoleon is like a stormy torrent which we are as yet unable to stop. Moscow will be the sponge that will suck him in."[53]

the beginning of the invasion, Smolensk in the middle of August. There was some sharp fighting but no major attempt at resistance. This strategy, which was dictated by necessity and which probably won the war, was regarded by many as treason, and the tsar and his generals were subject to unsparing criticism.[51]

Many Russians hailed Napoleon's troops as liberators. Once Russians realized, however, that the invaders would be just as oppressive as the old rulers, resistance tightened. As the French soldiers seized food for themselves and their horses from the peasants, the Russians fought back with guerrilla attacks. These hit-and-

Stopping Napoleon

Amid cries of treason, notes Tarle, Russian residents and troops fled Moscow:

Frightened, confused, silent throngs of those Muscovites who had not yet been able to leave crowded the streets and public squares, watching the departing troops. The soldiers marched gloomily, silently, with their eyes downcast. Witnesses tell us that some among the rank-and-file were weeping.[54]

Napoleon took Moscow without a fight. Napoleon expected Alexander I to meet him and accept defeat.

But soon Napoleon began hearing reports from his troops that he could not believe. Moscow was not only empty, it was on fire. Just before leaving, the governor of the region had ordered all fire pumps removed and fires started. For five days the city burned uncontrollably. Napoleon

Napoleon retreats from Moscow after losing much of his army to guerrilla attacks, illness, and hunger.

had taken Moscow. But what had it gained him? Ashes and cinders.

For the next month Napoleon held Moscow, until he realized his great triumph was a hollow victory. The Russians refused to negotiate. Napoleon knew that even he did not have enough troops to chase the Russians all the way to the Pacific Ocean. Nor could he stay in Moscow forever. On October 19 Napoleon and his undefeated army began to retreat.

As the retreat began, it became obvious how the months of marching and fighting had exhausted Napoleon's soldiers. Many became ill. The number of deaths mounted. Russian guerrilla attacks continued, making gathering food nearly impossible. By the beginning of November, says Markham, "the army was disintegrating through sheer hunger."[55]

Then, on November 5, the snows began. Cold and snow added to hunger, illness, and attacks to ravage the once mighty French army. By the end of November the orderly retreat had disintegrated into complete disorder. In late December the last of Napoleon's troops reached home. Fewer than forty thousand troops had survived.

The Russians, aided by the cold, had stopped Napoleon, the most powerful European ruler to that time. Within three years his empire would be destroyed and he would be imprisoned. In stopping Napoleon, the Russians had changed the course of European history.

Alexander I's Death

In November 1825 Alexander I died, creating a controversy over who should succeed him. He had written a note declaring that his successor would be his youngest brother, Nicholas, rather than Constantine, the middle brother.

However, when Alexander died, the note was never made public. Only a few close advisers knew about it. Although Constantine did not want to be tsar, citi-

Moscow on Fire

The burning of Moscow before the French could occupy it startled the invaders. Here is how Baron Claude-François de Méneval, of the French troops, recalled the events in his book Memoirs to Serve for the History of Napoleon I. *This excerpt is taken from John Carey's* Eyewitness to History.

"Hardly had the Emperor [Napoleon] entered the Kremlin than fire broke out in the Kitaigorod, or Chinese city, an immense bazaar, surrounded by porticoes [roofs supported by columns], in which were heaped up, in large shops or in cellars, the entrances to which were placed in the middle of the streets, precious goods of every kind, such as shawls, furs, Indian and Chinese tissues. Fruitless efforts were made to extinguish the flames, and burning of the bazaar became the signal for a general conflagration [great fire] in the city. The conflagration, spreading rapidly, devoured three-quarters of Moscow in three days. Each moment one saw smoke followed by flames breaking out of houses which had remained intact and in the end the fire broke out in every house in the city. The town was one mighty furnace from which sheaves of fire burst heavenwards lighting up the horizon with the glaring flames and spreading a burning heat. These masses of flame, mingling together, were rapidly caught up by a strong wind which spread them in every direction. They were accompanied by a succession of whistling noises and explosions caused by the falling walls and the explosion of inflammable materials which were stored in the shops and houses. To these roaring noises, to these sinister outbreaks added themselves the cries and yells of the wretched people who were caught by the flames in the houses which they had entered to pillage [rob] and which many escaped only to perish in the streets which formed a blazing labyrinth from which all escape was impossible. Motionless and in the silence of stupor we looked on at this horrible and magnificent spectacle, with the feeling of our absolute helplessness to render any assistance."

zens, guards, and palace officials began taking an oath of allegiance to Constantine. They assumed that he, as the oldest surviving brother, was the rightful heir. Constantine repeated that he did not want to become tsar. If anyone tried to make him, he would "leave Warsaw only to retire to some greater distance"[56] from Moscow, according to Walsh.

For three weeks Russia had no clear tsar. Nobles who served in the palace and the military lined up in support of Nicholas or Constantine, hoping to back the man who would eventually take power.

Roots of Revolution

In St. Petersburg one group of military officers openly denounced Nicholas I and declared their support for Constantine. But these officers had no great loyalty to Constantine. Rather, according to historian Edward Crankshaw, they had a bigger goal. Years earlier as young soldiers, many had fought against Napoleon's troops in eastern Europe. There they had seen ordinary citizens reading newspapers, debating politics, and eating until full. Then they returned to a Russia of illiteracy, fear, and hunger. These officers realized that Russia needed not just small reforms, but radical change. In the confusion about who was the rightful tsar, the officers decided to act. According to author Edward Crankshaw, they disagreed over what change they wanted: "Some wanted to force a constitution on the Tsar, others to depose him and proclaim a republic, others to kill him. They were united only in their determination to put an end to autocratic rule."[57] In supporting Constantine,

then, the officers' real goal was to get rid of the absolute power of the tsar. They wanted a revolution.

Two Uprisings

Realizing that such an aim was too radical to win the support of most soldiers, the rebel officers did not declare their revolutionary intentions. To attract soldiers to their cause, they promised "easier conditions and more pay,"[58] according to Crankshaw. On December 14 about three thousand soldiers supporting the rebel officers met at a square in St. Petersburg. They declared their allegiance to Constantine. Just by standing there, they challenged Nicholas's authority as tsar.

The soldiers stayed all day long, refusing to leave. The government feared that other soldiers would join them. Hoping to negotiate a settlement, government representatives tried to approach the soldiers more than once. Each time, hotheaded soldiers who wanted no negotiations fired on them. Finally, after a long, chilly day of attempted negotiations and a few scattered deaths, a frustrated general told the new tsar, Nicholas I, "Sire, sweep the square with gun-fire or abdicate [give up power]."[59] Nicholas I listened. Then Nicholas gave the order to fire. Reports Crankshaw:

> After warning shots the three guns fired straight into the mass over open sights. At once all was chaos. Bloody reality broke in with a shock that was all the greater for being withheld so long. There was no resistance, the great crowd broke and fled. Dead and wounded lay scattered on the square. More shots tore into the fleeing mass as

it tried to break out of the square down narrow streets. Others ran for the ice on the Neva, where they tried to regroup. But the gunners went on, now using cannon-balls to smash the ice and the bodies of the defeated. Nobody ever knew how many were killed as the darkness closed in on the stone heart of the great city. But all that night the police went silently about collecting the corpses and pushing them down with poles through holes in the ice—and with them many of the wounded.[60]

Just as the rebels in St. Petersburg were being crushed, a related uprising started in Kiev. The two groups of rebels were led by military officers who knew each other and shared a sense that Russia needed drastic change. While the groups had been in contact secretly, they had only loosely coordinated their plans to rebel. The Kiev group, besides being small and disorganized, included traitors who leaked the plans just as the rebellion was to begin. Within days the leaders of the Kiev uprising were captured.

The Legacy of the Decembrist Revolt

The uprisings in St. Petersburg and Kiev became known as the Decembrist Revolt. Five leaders were executed. Another 280 were exiled to Siberia. The event was over. As quoted by historian Charques, Nicholas I vowed, "Revolution stands on the threshold of Russia, but I swear it will never enter Russia while my breath lasts."[61]

From the end of the Decembrist Revolt onward, Nicholas I tried to keep his

Nicholas I vowed that a Russian revolution would not occur during his reign. When the Decembrist Revolt broke out, Tsar Nicholas crushed the rebellion and executed its leaders.

vow. Ever fearful of another uprising, he organized a private army of spies and soldiers. Their goal was to seek out and arrest anyone who dared challenge his power. Though not as needlessly cruel as Ivan the Terrible or Peter the Great, he was ruthless. He became known as Nicholas the Flogger, says Charques, for his "brutal authoritarianism."[62] He wanted the entire country regimented—right down to the mustaches that men wore. According to Cowles, "only the army had the right to wear mustaches, and all mustaches had to be black, dyed if necessary."[63]

But despite Nicholas I's efforts, thoughts of revolution did not die with the Decembrist Revolt. Russians who questioned the system of tsarist rule remembered those who died or suffered years in exile. They became martyrs—symbols of a movement. Walsh quotes one later revolutionary, Aleksandr Herzen, who said,

> The heritage we received from the Decembrists was the awakened feeling of human dignity, the striving for independence, the hatred of slavery, the respect for Western Europe and for the Revolution, the faith in the possibility of an upheaval in Russia, and the passionate desire to take part in it.[64]

The Decembrists failed in their revolt, but they had become powerful in their defeat. Even Nicholas I's police state could not destroy the movement they started. Almost a century later this movement would topple the tsarist system.

As Russian politics were slowly beginning to change, so was the Russian economy. For example, Russia's trade with other countries was increasing. Grain exports from Russia doubled between the late 1830s and the late 1840s. Most of the wheat, rye, and other crops that Russia exported went to the growing cities of Europe. With the increase in trade came the development of a more extensive transportation network. By 1870 rail lines linked Moscow to St. Petersburg on the Baltic Sea, to Odessa on the Black Sea, and to Orenburg on the Ural River. Other rail lines connected the iron ore fields in the Ural Mountains near Ekaterinburg to rivers that reached Archangel, or Arkhangelsk, on the White Sea. These rail lines and others were financed primarily by the government.

The Daydreamer

Russian peasants seemed trapped in poverty. The following folktale reflects one viewpoint about why they could not escape poverty. It is from a collection entitled Russian Fairy Tales *compiled by Aleksandr Afanas'ev and translated by Norbert Guterman.*

"A poor peasant walking in a field saw a hare under a bush and was overjoyed. He said: 'Now I'm in luck! I will catch this hare, kill him with a whip, and sell him for twelve kopecks [a unit of money]. For that money I will buy a sow, and she will bring me twelve piglets; the piglets will grow up and each bring twelve piglets; I will slaughter them all, and have a barnful of meat. I will sell the meat, and with the money will set up housekeeping and get married. My wife will bear me two sons, Vaska and Vanka. The children will plow the field, and I will sit by the window and give orders. "Hey, you boys!" I will cry. "Vaska and Vanka! Don't overwork your laborers; apparently you yourselves have never known poverty!"' And the peasant shouted these words so loudly that the hare was startled and ran away, and his house with all his riches and his wife, and his children were lost."

Peasant life was also beginning to change. For centuries most Russian peasants made the clothes, boots, candles, tools, and other items they needed. Beginning in the 1800s many peasants began making extra items to sell to merchants. The merchants, in turn, would sell the goods in Moscow, Kiev, or another city. With the money they earned, a peasant family could then buy extra food or better clothes. Peasants were becoming dependent on selling and buying goods.

Peasants, though, were not efficient producers. Making goods by hand was slow. To be more productive, peasants needed machines driven by water or steam power, such as power looms for making cloth. So merchants or nobles began to buy machines and hire workers, or assign serfs, to operate them. Early Russian factories were generally small and located in rural areas. They often produced textiles, carpets, or shoes. Between 1825 and 1860 the number of factory workers in Russia grew from about 200,000 people to about 565,000. The shift from making goods by hand to making them with power-driven machines, in Russia and elsewhere, is called the Industrial Revolution.

The Industrial Revolution

With the Industrial Revolution came a greater demand for educated citizens. Negotiating trade deals, supervising factories, and running railroads required individuals who could read and write well enough to follow business contracts, timetables, and government regulations. The Russian educational system began expanding in the 1800s, but it was tiny compared to that of the United States or western Europe. Outside of cities, schools were rare. And by the mid-1800s Russia had only five universities. Their total enrollment was between three and four thousand. Almost all students were the children of nobles or of military officers.

Despite the growth of trade, transportation, and education, Russia's economy lagged far behind those of Europe and the United States. Comparing the governments of Russia and the United States suggests why. The United States had a strong system of state and local governments. These lower levels of government built local roads and canals, opened schools in every community, and promoted small businesses. Russia had almost no regional or local governments to do these tasks. What the tsar's government did not do, no one did. As economic historian Colin White concluded, "In contrast to eighteenth and nineteenth century America, Russia was undergoverned."[65]

Russia's Cultural Awakening

By the mid-1800s Russia's educated class, though small, was growing. And with its growth came new cultural developments. For the first time Russian writers, composers, and intellectuals became prominent outside of Russia. For example, in literature, Aleksandr Pushkin, who lived from 1799 to 1837, wrote poetry, plays, and novels that won wide acclaim in Europe and the United States. Even such a talented artist as Pushkin, though, could not avoid government repression. He was temporarily exiled twice for his association with political dissenters. After 1826

The Intellectuals

Writer Aleksandr Pushkin, a known associate of political dissenters, was exiled twice. His works offended Russia's government leaders and were censored.

Nicholas I took personal responsibility for censoring what Pushkin wrote. During the eighty years following Pushkin's death, he was followed by a host of brilliant Russian writers. Among the best known are Fyodor Dostoyevsky, Leo Tolstoy, and Anton Chekhov.

In music, Mikhail Glinka, who lived from 1804 to 1857, became the first significant Russian composer of orchestral music. Though influenced by German and French composers, his emotional, expressive music made extensive use of Russian folk melodies. These melodies gave his works a distinctive Russian sound. Famous Russian composers after Glinka included Aleksandr Borodin, Nikolay Rimsky-Korsakov, Pyotr (Peter) Tchaikovsky, and Igor Stravinsky.

Another aspect of the cultural awakening was the growth of an intellectual class, people whose primary activity was teaching in universities or writing books, essays, and articles. The most influential of these intellectuals was Aleksandr Herzen. Historian Isaiah Berlin called him "the most realistic, sensitive, penetrating and convincing witness to the social life and the social issues of his own time."[66] In 1834 he was exiled for six years because he had joined a group of political dissenters. After his exile he used money he inherited from his nobleman father to leave Russia. Only from outside the country, he realized, could he criticize the government freely. From London he published a journal, *The Bell*. Its circulation never exceeded three thousand, and he published it for only ten years, but it was tremendously influential. Even the tsar read it. Officials in Russia, rather than risk criticizing a policy, would smuggle information, gossip, and stories to Herzen to print. They knew they could reach a powerful, if small, audience in Russia through him.

Herzen wanted Russia to copy moderate reforms common in western Europe: more schools, freedom of the press, support for scientific study, and an end to corporal punishments such as whipping. He also wanted radical reform: an end to serfdom. These changes, he hoped, would make Russia a free, democratic country. Herzen and other Russian intellectuals who believed that Russia could learn much from western Europe became known as Westerners.

One aspect of western European life that Herzen did not want Russia to copy

Peasant Conservatism

"Nekhlyudov walked into the hut. The uneven, grimy walls were in the kitchen corner covered with all kinds of rags and clothes, while the corner of honour was literally red with cockroaches that swarmed about the images and benches. In the middle of this black, ill-smelling, eighteen-foot hut there was a large crack in the ceiling, and although supports were put in two places, the ceiling was so bent that it threatened to fall down any minute.

[Nekhlyudov offers to allow Churis and his family to move to a new stone hut that has just been built in a new village. There Churis and his family will be safe, dry, and warm. Churis responds:]

'We shall be ruined, your Grace, if you insist upon our going there, completely ruined! It is a new place, an unknown place—' he repeated, with a melancholy, but firm, shake of his head. . . . 'Here is a cheery place, a gay place, and we are used to it, and to the road, and the pond, where the women wash the clothes and the cattle go to water; and all our peasant surroundings have been here since time immemorial,—and the threshing-floor, the garden, and the willows that my parents have set out. My grandfather and father have given their souls to God here, and I ask nothing else, your Grace, but to be able to end my days here. . . . Drive us not from our nest, sir.'"

was its economic system, capitalism. Under capitalism, land and factories are privately owned. Herzen thought that capitalism allowed workers to be treated just as brutally as serfs were. Herzen supported a form of socialism, an economic system in which land, factories, and businesses are owned by those who work on or in them. He praised the Russian peasants, because they had always farmed their land collectively.

Most Russian intellectuals shared Herzen's dislike of capitalism and his appreciation of Russian peasant life. However, some thought that western Europe had nothing to teach Russia. Democracy and freedom, they said, were alien to Russian culture. Science, they charged, threatened to undermine the Russian Orthodox Church. These intellectuals urged Russians to look not to the west, but to their Slavic past for guidance. Hence, they became known as Slavophiles. They believed that the peasant village, the tsar, and the Russian Orthodox Church provided the foundation of a strong Russia. One of the leaders of the Slavophiles was A. S. Khomyakov, a good friend of Herzen's.

A third group of Russian intellectuals disagreed with both the Westerners and the Slavophiles. Men such as N. G. Chernyshevsky believed that neither western Europe nor Russia's distant past could provide a guide to the future. What they wanted—besides change—is hard to say. Because they seemed to believe in nothing, they were labeled Nihilists. This name is based on the Latin word *nihil*, which means "nothing."

The debates among the Westerners, Slavophiles, and Nihilists were limited. Few Russians could read the novels, magazine essays, or newspaper articles they wrote. Fewer still were interested. In addition, the intellectuals lived under the constant threat of imprisonment or exile. Since they had to avoid sensitive political subjects, they focused their debates on history and literature. For example, while Westerners praised Peter the Great for his progressive reforms, Slavophiles attacked him for undermining traditional Russian customs. Despite these limits, the debates marked a new development in Russia. For the first time in Russian history, an educated class was debating the future of Russian society. Over the next several decades, as the number of educated Russians increased, so would their influence. Many would continue to reject capitalism as the solution to Russian problems.

The Crimean War

The debates among Westerners, Slavophiles, and Nihilists occurred at a time when Russians were proud of their army. Though a poor country, Russia had a large and powerful military. The threat of using this military gave Russia political power. Between the defeat of Napoleon in 1812 and the 1850s, Russia used its influence to oppose democratic uprisings throughout eastern and central Europe. In 1849, for example, two hundred thousand Russian troops helped crush a rebellion by Hungarians living in the Austrian Empire. The rebels, led by Lajos Kossuth, wanted the right to govern themselves within the empire.

Nicholas I hoped to use the Russian military to continue the expansion of Russia's empire. In 1853 Nicholas I sent military forces into the regions of Walachia and Moldavia. He said he was protecting Christians living under the Turkish Ottoman Empire. This small move, though, touched off a sharp reaction. France, Great Britain, and Austria feared Russian domination of the Middle East. They went to aid the Turks. The dispute escalated into the Crimean War.

Russia entered the war confidently. Yet the war was, in short, a disaster. The supposedly mighty Russian army lost battle after battle. According to Cowles, the Russians were humiliated:

> The Crimean roads were deep with mud and strewn with the carcasses of horses who had died from thirst and hunger, and whose rotting bodies spread a wave of epidemic. Medical supplies were almost non-existent;

A battle scene from the Crimean War, a devastating failure that caused many Russians to turn a critical eye on their country.

there was mould [mold] in the biscuits, weevil [beetles] in the salted meat; the water was tainted; the soldier's boots were falling to pieces. Yet everyone whispered of the great profits made by the Army Commissariat whose duty it was to feed the army.[67]

A young Leo Tolstoy, the man who would later became known as one of Russia's greatest writers, summarized the problems facing the Russians: "Senseless training, useless weapons, ill treatment, universal procrastination, ignorance, appalling hygiene and food, stifle the last spark of pride in a man."[68]

In February 1855 Nicholas I contracted pneumonia and died. His son and successor, Alexander II, quickly brought the losing war effort to an end. Approximately six hundred thousand people had died in the war—roughly the number of deaths in the Civil War in the United States. The treaty, signed in March 1856, cost Russia most of the land it had seized along the Danube River. In addition, Russia agreed not to fortify its ports on the Black Sea.

The treaty was not terribly harsh. However, says Florinsky, the war "exploded the myth of the invincible strength of the Russian military forces."[69] More than just a few intellectuals began asking questions. Why, many Russians wondered, was the country humiliated in this war? Why were Russian troops so poorly trained? Why were they so poorly equipped? Why were so many officials corrupt? What was wrong with Russia? Answering these questions would prompt one of the greatest changes in Russian history.

5 Reform and Reaction: 1856–1894

In the midst of the reign of Nicholas I, a nineteen-year-old noble and his advisers took a journey through Siberia. Though on a tight schedule, the young man demanded frequent stops. He wanted to visit with peasants. According to Crankshaw, "while officials exchanged despairing glances and railed at each other for mismanagement of the tour," the young man

> went into the wretched huts, chosen at random, and sat down on filthy stools in the dark and airless murk [gloom], seeing and feeling for himself the misery which encompassed so many millions of [Russians]. He received no words of complaint from them: none dared to speak. But he could see, and he could remember.[70]

That young noble was Tsar Nicholas I's son Alexander. When Alexander became tsar after his father's death in 1855, he did not forget what miserable lives the peasants led. Nor could he suppress the frequent explosions of peasant violence: Russia now averaged six new peasant uprisings each month. Finally, he could not ignore the lessons of the Crimean War: Russia was a pitifully weak giant of a country. Because of what he could not forget, suppress, or ignore, Alexander II con-

cluded that Russia must change. He decided to free the serfs, the peasants who served the nobles. These serfs were about half of all peasants. As he told a group of nobles, "it is better to abolish serfdom from above than await the time when it will begin to abolish itself from below."[71]

Realizing that discontent continued to exist among peasants and that violent uprisings were inevitable, Alexander II freed the serfs.

The Great Emancipation

Within a year of becoming tsar, Alexander II began appointing a variety of commissions to answer the many questions that ending serfdom raised. Should nobles be compensated for losing their serfs? If so, where would the money come from? Would serfs become landowners? Should they pay for land they received? How fast should changes occur? The commissions continued to debate until 1861. The serfs, those with the most at stake, had no representatives at these talks. Closed out of the discussion, the serfs continued to speak through protests, threats of violence against landlords, and small-scale rebellions.

Finally, in the spring of 1861, amidst a swirl of rumors about what he might really announce, Alexander II published the long-awaited decree: "The right of bondage over the peasants . . . is forever abolished."[72] This was the first in an impressive series of reforms. Through additional decrees over the next five years, all peasants, whether they labored for nobles or the government, became free. Emancipation freed over fifty million people. By comparison, the emancipation of slaves in the United States in the same decade was a small event. Only four million slaves were freed. The Tsar Liberator, as Alexander II became known, did not stop with freeing the peasants. He also pushed through a range of other changes. He revamped the judicial system, revised the tax code, and improved the education system. Each of these reforms attempted to make Russian life more free and open.

The 1861 decree ending serfdom was greeted with an outburst of enthusiasm. Historian Vernadsky quotes nineteen-year-old Prince Pyotr Kropotkin, who would later become a revolutionary leader, recalling the joy he saw: "Crowds of peasants and educated men stood in front of the palace, shouting harrahs [hurrahs], and the Tsar could not appear without being followed by demonstrative crowds running after his carriage."[73]

The serfs hoped that freedom would also bring them control of the land that they and their ancestors had worked. In order to achieve a compromise with the nobles who opposed abolition, though, Alexander II had made several decisions, including that the nobles could keep control of much of the land that the serfs had worked. In addition, they established a system in which newly freed peasants would have to pay for the land they did receive. According to Vaillant and Richards, "Only about one-third of the land to which they [the former serfs] felt entitled was made available to them, however, and it was not free. To buy land, they had to borrow money from the state, to be repaid in installments over forty-nine years."[74]

Most peasants found themselves poorer after emancipation than before it. They had less land to work and they had to pay for it. Though legally free, they felt as trapped as they had been as serfs. According to reformer Aleksandr Herzen: "The old serfdom was replaced by a new one."[75]

Outraged peasants rose in protest across Russia. Nearly two thousand rebellions rocked the country. This was as many as in the entire thirty-five years before emancipation. Their anger was directed primarily at the nobles. They believed that the tsar had tried to help them but that the nobles had prevented him from doing what he wished. In retrospect, abolishing

Emancipation

In his book Unfree Labor, historian Peter Kolchin compares American slavery and Russian serfdom. Though the two systems of bondage ended in the same decade, they ended in quite different ways.

"Emancipation in Russia, while momentous, represented less of a break with the past [than did emancipation in the United States]. Abolition of serfdom occurred internally (although from above) rather than by imposition of outside force; unlike southern [U.S.] planters, Russian pomeshchiki [a category of landowners] did not see their power and influence crushed by military defeat. Indeed, once the inevitability of change was clear to them, they played a major role in drafting and implementing the provisions of the emancipation settlement. As a result, emancipation, though representing a significant new departure for Russia, occurred within a broad framework of continuity. There was no radical attempt to give sudden equality to the ex-serfs or to break the social and economic hegemony [domination] of the pomeshchiki; peasants were still peasants and noblemen still noblemen in a highly stratified [layered] society. Russian emancipation, unlike southern, was undertaken with the interests of the masters at heart and involved both financial compensation to owners and measures to ensure their continued authority in the countryside. In this respect the Russian experience was typical of the emancipation process in most slave societies, from the British West Indies and Brazil to the northern United States; the unusual vehicle of southern emancipation—Civil War—brought with it unusual revolutionary potential as well."

serfdom was only the first step needed to reform Russian society. As long as one autocratic, or all-powerful, ruler and a small class of nobles dominated the country, the life of average Russians would not change.

The peasant rebellions encouraged a growing group of young radicals to believe in a revolution. As intellectual followers of Herzen, many of the young radicals were the sons or daughters of minor nobles or government officials. Most were from cities. Often they were university students or recent graduates. In general they had little contact with peasants. They wanted to replace tsarist rule with democracy, to reduce the power of the Russian Orthodox Church, and to provide more land to the peasants. And, like Herzen, they had an almost limitless faith in the wisdom and goodness of Russian peasants.

Radicals and Terrorists

In 1873 and 1874 many Russian radicals decided to take their message to the peasants. Nearly three thousand radicals moved to the villages and spread their revolutionary message. They went on their own; they were neither directed nor sent by any organization or leader. They simply went, filled with hope.

Some of the radicals thought that by giving fiery speeches in village after village they would inspire the peasants to rise in anger and overthrow the tsar.

Other radicals did not expect an immediate uprising. They wanted to educate the peasants gradually, preparing them for a revolution in the future. Instead of traveling from place to place, these radicals settled down in a village, offering peasants medical care or teaching children to read and write. Some of the radicals tried farmwork or carpentry—work requiring skills that they did not have. As they lived among the peasants, they tried to convince their neighbors of the need for revolution.

The peasants' reaction to the radicals, though, was not revolution. Rather, according to historian Berlin, the radicals were met with "mounting indifference, suspicion, resentment, and sometimes active hatred and resistance, on the part of their would-be beneficiaries [the peasants, who would benefit], who as often as not, handed them over to the police."[76] Hundreds of radicals were arrested by the police and jailed.

The radicals of 1873 and 1874 found that most peasants still believed in the tsar as their defender. Most peasants were also devout Christians, either as members of the Russian Orthodox Church or as members of a sect of Old Believers. They were not interested in the radicals' anticlerical message. And while peasants agreed with the radicals on the issue of redistributing the land, many did so primarily because they wanted more land for themselves. According to historian Avrahm Yarmolinsky, one peasant reacted to the demand for repartitioning the land among the peasants by declaring, "Won't that be great when we divide up the land! I'll hire two farmhands and live like a lord!"[77]

Some radicals became disenchanted with the peasants. They concluded that peasants were too tied to the tsar and the church to ever overthrow the system. Some other group would have to lead the revolution. Radicals who came to this conclusion, such as Georgy Plekhanov, were influenced by the ideas of German political philosopher Karl Marx. Marx believed that a free, democratic society could occur only through a revolution led by industrial workers. When the final end to tsarist rule came forty years later, Marxists and industrial workers played key roles.

Some radicals turned to violence to achieve their ends. Political terrorism, a minor strand in Russian political movements since the 1840s, quickly became a significant force. Its advocates hoped it would both pressure the government to change and provide inspiration to the Russian people. The most important terrorist group was the People's Will. Its members dedicated themselves to political assassinations. Though it consisted of at most a few dozen people, the People's

German political philosopher Karl Marx believed that a democratic society could be achieved only when the industrial workers revolted. Marx's revolutionary ideas inspired Russian radicals who opposed tsarist rule.

Will had a dramatic impact on Russian history over the next few decades.

The People's Will repeatedly attempted to assassinate the tsar. In March 1881 they finally succeeded. A bomb exploded under Alexander II's feet. The man who was known as the Tsar Liberator was dead. When he died, the era of reform was over.

Russification

Following the death of Alexander II, his son, Alexander III, took power. Alexander III ruled harshly, repealing the reforms his father had attempted to make. "Undoing almost everything his father had done, though he could not reestablish serfdom, he antagonized every class of Russian,"[78] concluded historian Henry Moscow.

Frustrated reformers turned to violence against Alexander III. A group of seven young men planned to kill the tsar. However, the plot was discovered and five of the men were hanged in 1887. Among them was Aleksandr Ulyanov. Thirty years later, Aleksandr's younger brother, Vladimir, would lead the revolution that would finally overthrow tsarist rule. By then Vladimir would be known to the world as Nikolay Lenin.

Alexander III often blamed Russia's problems on its ethnic groups. He had grown up during an era when nationalism had been spreading throughout Europe. According to nationalist beliefs, everyone in a country should share the same language, the same religion, and the same customs. Alexander III, influenced by the spirit of nationalism, wanted everyone in the country of Russia to be Russian.

However, only about half of the inhabitants were actually Russian. In the late 1800s Russia's population of one hundred million included fifty million Poles, Ukrainians, Latvians, Chechens, Armenians, Georgians, and members of dozens of other ethnic groups under Russian domination. These non-Russian ethnic groups often had their own languages, religions, and customs. And just as strongly as Alexander III wanted them to be Russian, many of them wanted to maintain their heritage.

The drive to Russify, or Russianize, all of these minority groups was a bitter, sometimes violent, process. People who did not speak Russian or did not attend the Russian Orthodox Church faced growing pressure to do so. Some laws reflected this pressure. For example, religious groups other than the Orthodox Church were banned from trying to recruit new members. In 1881 the government issued new regulations that allowed either the tsar or some of the tsar's chief advisers to declare a state of emergency in a region. According to Crankshaw, such a declaration allowed officials to jail people without a trial, fine individuals, prohibit public gatherings, and close down businesses. These laws gave the government new powers to use whenever it wanted to punish a minority that did not seem eager to adopt the Russian language and religion.

Alexander III blamed Russia's problems on its wide variety of ethnic groups, and he strove to make them conform to the Russian language, church, and customs.

Anti-Semitism

No group suffered more than the five million Jews living in southwestern Russia. The government's efforts at Russification intensified the anti-Semitism that many Russians had long felt. Anti-Semites justified their hatred by blaming Jews for murdering Jesus. Further, they claimed, Jews led an international conspiracy that controlled the world economy and kept Russia poor. One of the tsar's advisers thought Russia should eliminate all Jews. He hoped that one-third of Russian Jews could be converted to Christianity. Another third could be pushed out of the country. The final third, he concluded, would have to be killed.

Under Alexander III the Russian government passed several restrictions on Jews. For example, the government limited the number of Jews entering high school. According to Chaim Weizmann, who would become the first president of Israel (1949–1952), "in a Jewish population numbering perhaps tens of thousands [in a region], only four or five or six Jewish students would be admitted." However, he points out, the wealthy could sometimes get around the law. The number of Jews allowed into school was limited to a percentage of the number of students who took the entrance exams. So, explains Weizmann, by increasing the number of students taking the exams, more Jews could enter school. "There were occasions," recalled Weizmann, "when a rich Jew would hire ten non-Jewish candidates at times rather oddly selected to sit for the entrance examination at the local school, and thus make room for one Jewish pupil—needless to say, his own son or a protege."[79]

The Duty to Rebel

Sentenced to die for his role in a failed assassination attempt against Alexander III, Aleksandr Ulyanov was granted a final meeting with his mother. In his book Black Night, White Snow, *journalist Harrison Salisbury described Ulyanov's meeting with his mother.*

"On April 1, two weeks before delivering his final speech, Ulyanov had been permitted a meeting with his mother, Mariya Alexandrovna. The Czar gave his permission because he thought the interview would reveal to the despairing woman the 'true nature' of her son. A prison official was unobtrusively present. Mother and son wept, Alexander begging his mother to forgive him for bringing her such grief. Then he talked of the dictatorial, repressive regime which held the country in thrall [bondage] and of the duty, as he saw it, of every honest man to fight for the liberation of Russia.

'Yes,' sighed his mother, 'but with such terrible means!'

'But,' replied Alexander in the classic form in which the question had been asked by so many generations of young Russians, '*Chto delat?* What is there to do, Mama, when there are no other means?'"

More serious than these quotas, though, were the waves of violent attacks on Jews called pogroms. Mobs beat Jews, burned their homes to the ground, and ransacked their synagogues. They murdered thousands of Jews. Prince Urusov was a noble who investigated one pogrom and reported that mobs would "beat and plunder the Jews in the name of the Orthodox Church, in defence of the orthodox people, and for the glory of the autocratic Russian Czar."[80]

The role of local authorities in pogroms was mixed. On one hand, many local leaders joined with some nobles and clergy in publicly condemning the burning, beating, and killing as violations of the law. On the other hand, local authorities often waited a few days before stopping the violence. By waiting to take action, a local government could indicate its quiet support for the pogroms. Crankshaw says that Tsar Alexander III spoke for many in the government when he admitted, "In my heart, I am very glad when they [common citizens] beat the Jews, even though this practice cannot be permitted."[81]

One of the worst pogroms occurred in Kishinev, a city 125 miles north of the Black Sea. It happened in the spring of 1903 at the time of Easter and Passover. According to historian W. Bruce Lincoln, one of the events that touched off the pogrom was the death of a young girl:

Weizmann on Self-Defense

Chaim Weizmann was a Jew who grew up in Russia in the late 1800s. He was teaching school and attending a university in Germany when he heard about the pogrom at Kishinev in 1903. In his autobiography Trial and Error, *he describes his reaction.*

"Perhaps the most tormenting feature of the Kishinev pogrom was the fact that the Jews had allowed themselves to be slaughtered like sheep, without offering general resistance. In spite of the wild pogrom, agitation of Krushevan [a leader of the pogrom], they had refused to believe in the possibility of a massacre carried out under the aegis [authority] of the Government; and the attack which occurred in the midst of the last sacred days of Passover overwhelmed them. . . .

I had intended to proceed from Warsaw to Geneva. I abandoned my classes, such as they were, and returned to the Pale [Jewish settlement]. Together with friends and acquaintances I proceeded to organize self-defense groups in all the larger Jewish centers. Not long afterward, when a pogrom broke out in Homel, not far from Pinsk, the hooligans were suddenly confronted by a strongly organized Jewish self-defense corps. Again the military interfered, and did its best to disarm the Jews; but at least the self-defense had broken the first wave of the attack, which was not able to gather again its original momentum. Thus, throughout the Pale, an inverted [upside down] guerrilla warfare spread, between the Jews and the Russian authorities, the former trying to maintain order, the latter encouraging disorder. The Jews grew more and more exasperated and our life therefore more and more intolerable."

Chaim Weizmann, who served as the first president of Israel from 1948 to 1952, encouraged Jewish people to defend themselves against attacks by Russian authorities.

*Jewish victims of the pogroms. Between 1880 and 1914 about one million Jews
fled Russia to escape the violence of the mob attacks.*

Smoldering popular suspicion grew more intense on Easter eve, when a Christian servant girl died in Kishinev's Jewish hospital under mysterious circumstances. It turned out that she had poisoned herself and had died despite desperate efforts by her Jewish employer to save her, but popular opinion preferred to believe that she . . . had become a victim of ritual sacrifice [believed to be practiced by Jews].[82]

By noon on Easter, bands of Christians were attacking Jews throughout the city. The result: forty-five deaths, several hundred injuries, and over a thousand homes and shops attacked.

The pogroms drove many Jews away. Between 1880 and 1914 about one million Jews fled Russia. Most settled in western Europe and the United States. Other Jews stayed. Between the 1800s and 1917 many of these sought to defend themselves by joining the Bund, a Jewish socialist reform movement. Joining this movement, or any political movement, was risky. The dangers of continued pogroms, though, made many feel that the risk was worth it. The Bund pushed for laws that would protect all Russian citizens. By 1917 the Bund became a significant force for reform in Russia.

Industrialization

While Alexander III's policy of Russification created problems for many people, his economic policies created new opportunities for them. With strong support from the tsar and his ministers, the slow expansion of trade, transportation, and factory production that had begun in the mid-1800s became more rapid in the late 1800s. For example, iron production increased from about 800,000 tons in 1870 to almost 2 million tons in 1890. Coal production went from 800,000 tons to over 5 million tons in the same period. In 1891 the country had about 22,000 miles of railroad track. By 1901 it had added another 15,000 miles. In the early 1900s this growth continued, though not quite as rapidly. The government promoted expansion by building railroads, financially aiding private companies, and encouraging foreigners to invest in Russia.

This expansion created jobs for some poverty-stricken Russians. They moved to cities to take jobs in ever larger factories. Russia's urban population increased from 6 million in 1863 to 18.6 million in 1914. However, Russia remained poor. In the late 1800s wealth per inhabitant was less than four hundred dollars in Russia. In much of Europe it was over eight hundred dollars. In Great Britain and the United States, it was over sixteen hundred dollars. Russia's high death rate reflected this poverty. In many communities half of the children died by the age of five.

Peasants who took industrial jobs still had hard lives. Wages were low. In 1910, for example, they were only half what British workers earned. They were even lower for women than for men. Sometimes wages were paid only twice a year.

People worked long days. In St. Petersburg a typical workday lasted between thirteen and seventeen hours. In 1897 a law limited the workday to eleven and a half hours. Later laws reduced the workday further. However, laws were enforced loosely. Meals were simple. Workers often ate rye bread three meals a day, with cabbage soup at noon and in the evening.

One shop owner pointed out that he was not to blame for abusing his workers: "Competition forces me to use as much cheap and unpaid labor as I can."[83] If he did not push his workers as hard as others did, he and his employees would soon be out of business. As Herzen and other reformers had warned in the 1840s, in a competitive economy acting humanely meant going broke.

At least some factory owners regretted how miserably they treated their workers. According to historians Kyril Fitzlyon and Tatiana Browning,

Timofey Morozov, Russia's leading textile manufacturer, railway magnate [wealthy owner], banker . . . spent his nights on his knees, praying God to forgive him his harsh treatment of his employees. He knew of no other way of dealing with men in this world, but did not wish to jeopardize his chances in the next.[84]

Despite the hardships, businesses had little difficulty finding hungry peasants willing to work for them. That people found the long hours, low pay, and harsh conditions of a factory attractive suggests how hard life was for peasants.

The Trans-Siberian Railway

The largest industrial project of this period and the one that hired thousands of

Female Factory Workers

Working conditions in factories were horrendous. However, earning a paycheck provided many women with greater freedom than ever before. Historian Barbara Alpern Engel, in an article in the journal Russian History, *describes some of the changes in male-female relationships that developed with factory work.*

"Factory labor also gave a woman a somewhat greater say in the choice of a marital partner, and forced marriage, strictly speaking, had become relatively rare. Still a girl never enjoyed as much say as the boys did, because parents gave their boys more leeway [choice]. They usually presented a son with the possibilities, or advised him to look around for himself; in either case, his choice was decisive, and the parents only sanctioned [approved] it. By contrast, the maiden's parents chose her spouse, and if she preferred someone else, they would try to talk her out of it, and usually, they would get their way. Parents in Melenki district of Vladimir province rarely even asked their daughters whether or not they consented to a match, 'so that a girl who lives at the factory does not know to whom they have betrothed [engaged] her, and only when she comes home do they tell her.' On the other hand, if a girl were really determined to marry someone, and insisted upon her choice, she would usually get her way. And it was relatively common for a girl to change her mind, and to reject the suitor before the wedding.

Earning their own wage made some wives more self-assertive, too. There is considerable evidence of married women's unruliness, and even more evidence of the anxieties it evoked [caused] in men. In peasant households, a man was supposed to control his wife and to ensure she behaved properly, if necessary by beating her. It was rare for the community to intervene in a marriage on behalf of a husband, or for him to complain to village authorities or to turn to the volost [local] court for help in handling his wife. When that happened, it was a sure sign that the man had lost control. Evidence that men had indeed lost control appears repeatedly in the *volost'* court records from industrial districts as early as the 1870s. . . . In Shuia, the peasants claimed that because women could no longer be beaten, they no longer feared anyone, and had become drunken and dissolute [wild]. 'Factory life has spoiled the women completely.'"

workers was the building of the Trans-Siberian Railway. This three-thousand-mile line linked western Russia with the Pacific Ocean. Construction began in 1891. It was built with the same ruthless disregard for life that characterized the construction of St. Petersburg almost two centuries earlier. Workers often labored seventeen hours a day. One newspaper account claimed that workers were given "putrid meat and bread that was so badly spoiled that even the local pigs would not eat it!" A group of workers lamented, "This ain't construction. It's a struggle, a war to the death."[85]

Yet the completion of the railway in 1904 opened up Siberia to development. The region's dazzling mineral resources—diamonds, rubies, coal, oil—spurred Russian economic growth in the 1900s. Siberia also became an ideal place to exile political opponents and criminals. Instead of sending individuals to prison, the government would send them to work camps in Siberia. There, often in frigid cold, they would work in mines or on construction projects. This forced labor helped develop the region.

The construction of the Trans-Siberian Railway and of other rail lines, roads, and factories required huge investments. To generate the money to pay for these projects, Russia needed to sell goods to other countries. So the Russian government followed tax and trade policies designed to

More than four hundred thousand Russians died of starvation during the famine of 1891–1892. Here, peasants receive soup provided by the government.

promote exports. These policies were particularly successful for wheat, rye, and other food items. By 1890 Russian grain exports were increasing, but the peasants had virtually no grain in reserve.

Famine

In the winter of 1890–1891 little snow fell on Russia or most of Europe. Then, in the spring of 1891, little rain fell. As evidence of drought increased, the price of grain rose throughout Europe and Russia. By May, Russian government officials began fearing widespread famine.

Some officials wanted to reduce taxes and limit grain exports to prevent massive starvation in Russia. Others, supported by grain merchants, thought Russia should profit from the rising prices in Europe and sell as much grain as it could. To the powerful finance minister, Ivan Vyshne-gradskii, the answer was simple: "We may not eat enough, but we will export."[86] With Vyshnegradskii's support, grain exports increased during the first six months of 1891. As conditions worsened, pressure to stop exports increased. By the time a ban on the export of rye took effect in the middle of August, thirty-six million Russians "were on the verge of starvation,"[87] according to Lincoln.

The government then made heroic efforts to distribute the grain remaining in the country to those in need. Despite sincere and exhaustive efforts, moving grain around Russia was slow. More than four hundred thousand Russians died before the famine ended in the fall of 1892.

As Russian peasants starved to death, the grain they had raised was shipped to those who could afford to buy it. This brutal lesson in market economics was not lost on many Russians. It would help lead to a revolution with far greater consequences than even the freeing of the peasants.

6 The End of Tsarist Rule: 1894–1917

"What am I going to do? What is going to happen to me . . . to all of Russia? I am not prepared to be a Tsar. I never wanted to become one." So said Nicholas II when he heard he would be tsar in 1894 after his father, Alexander III, died from kidney disease. It was, Nicholas II lamented, "the worst thing that could have happened to me, the thing I had been dreading so much all my life,"[88] according to historians Fitzlyon and Browning.

Few reigns in Russian history started so badly. As part of Nicholas II's coronation party, five hundred thousand people were gathered on a field outside Moscow. They were offered free drinks in souvenir cups. Somehow a rumor started that the cups were running out. As the rumor spread, the crowd became panicked and unruly, attempting to get a cup before the supply ran out. In the panic, as many as two thousand people were trampled to death.

Out of respect for those who died, Nicholas II wanted to cancel the rest of the scheduled coronation festivities. However, his advisers convinced him to attend a large diplomatic dinner with the French ambassador that evening. By continuing to celebrate after so many people had died, Nicholas II gained a reputation as a cruel, heartless man.

While neither cruel nor heartless, Nicholas II had no inclination to lead Russia toward the type of democratic reforms sweeping other countries. Following the lead of New Zealand and Australia, the United States and several European countries passed reforms to increase popular participation in government. In Russia, though, Nicholas II branded even small steps toward democracy "senseless dreams." He vowed to "uphold the principle of autocracy as firmly and as unflinchingly as my late unforgettable father."[89]

War with Japan

During his first ten years as tsar, Nicholas II faced widespread unrest. Every segment of society wanted change. Peasants rioted to protest their poverty; factory workers struck against oppressive working conditions; intellectuals demanded representative government. Rumors of revolution filled the air. Journalist Harrison Salisbury quotes V. K. Plehve, one of the tsar's top advisers: "In order to hold back the Revolution we need a small victorious war."[90]

Russia did indeed find its small war. While expanding eastward, Russia ran up against a rival, Japan, for control over Korea and Manchuria in northern China. The resulting military conflict was called the Russo-Japanese War.

The Russians assumed they would win easily. A gigantic country, Russia had far more resources to draw on than did tiny Japan. Russians also believed that they, as white Europeans, were racially superior to the Japanese. They believed that their natural superiority would win the war for them.

Yet from the first the war went badly for Russia. In February 1904 the Japanese surprised the Russians and defeated them at Port Arthur in Manchuria. Other defeats followed. By the end of 1904 many Russians realized they were going to lose the war. Walsh would summarize the Russian record as one of "repeated defeats relieved only by individual acts of heroism."[91]

Bloody Sunday

The defeats by Japan were only part of the problems facing the tsar and Russia. No matter how much Nicholas II refused to recognize it, things were changing. People could no longer tolerate their desperate living conditions. In January 1905 two hundred thousand Russians met in St. Petersburg to deliver a petition to the tsar. The marchers dressed in their best clothes and carried pictures of the tsar, whom they still respected even if they did not like him. Although the petition was vague, it called for an eight-hour workday and for an increase in wages.

The marchers were not radicals inspired by the Decembrists to overthrow tsarist rule. Rather, these Russians believed that the tsar was their protector.

They believed the tsar would prevent the suffering caused by oppressive landlords, ruthless factory owners, and corrupt bureaucrats. As the vast crowd assembled, the government panicked. It stationed thousands of troops around the city.

The protesters and the troops met on Sunday, January 22, 1905. The meeting quickly became violent. According to historian Moscow, "From all over St. Petersburg orderly processions carrying sacred icons and singing religious and patriotic songs converged on the Winter Palace. Troops which the government had posted to stop them opened fire."[92] One observer noted that even "little boys who had climbed the trees to watch what was going on were shot down like birds."[93] At least 150—maybe as many as 1,000—people died in what became known as Bloody Sunday.

For many Russians Bloody Sunday was a turning point. On that single day, claimed one Russian observer, momentum in Russian history shifted:

> Even on the morning of [Bloody Sunday], filled with belief in the Czar these masses were not ready for revolution. But by evening with the cry: "No longer do we have a Czar" they were ready to act. They rose against the autocrat. They began the revolution.[94]

For many Russians, by its actions on Bloody Sunday the government lost its right to rule them. It would never regain that right. The movement to end tsarist rule that began with the Decembrists suddenly had a broad base.

Over the next several months, over one thousand peasant uprisings rocked the country. The real centers of unrest were the cities. In Moscow, St. Petersburg, and elsewhere, industrial workers were

In St. Petersburg, Russian troops attack protesters who have come to deliver a petition to the tsar. As many as a thousand protesters were killed in what became known as Bloody Sunday.

striking and protesting against the government. The forty years of effort by intellectuals to spread revolutionary ideas in cities were finally showing results. Industrial workers were increasingly seeing themselves as the class that would lead the liberation of Russia.

Although Nicholas II reacted to this massive unrest by allowing some reform, including an elected legislature called the Duma, to advise him, the people were no longer patient and continued their protest. Nicholas and his government reacted just as previous tsars and their governments had reacted to protests. According to Lincoln,

Everywhere, troops fired upon striking workers. Sixty-five were killed and wounded in Stavropol, another forty in Nizhnii-Novgorod, and thirty-five more in Novorossiisk. In Belostok, the figure rose to over a hundred, and so it went throughout the summer.[95]

During the spring and summer of 1905, news from the war with Japan made the government even less popular. Each lost battle was a bitter blow to Russian pride. Nicholas II decided to end the disastrous war. Japan, not wanting to overextend itself, was also ready for peace. In September 1905 Russia and Japan signed a peace treaty. Japan won control of Korea and some land and key railways in Manchuria.

Ending the war, though, did not increase Nicholas's popularity or effectiveness to rule. In October a railroad strike paralyzed the entire country. In December a general strike shut down Moscow. In just one neighborhood in Moscow, one thousand citizens died in street fights against government soldiers. In Odessa, a port on the Black Sea, nearly two thousand citizens and soldiers died in clashes with one another. Between October 1905 and July

Petition to the Tsar

Russian workers in St. Petersburg marched to the Winter Palace in January 1905 hoping to give the tsar a petition asking for his help. The following is a portion of this petition, as quoted in Harrison Salisbury's Black Night, White Snow.

"We workers and residents of the city of St. Petersburg, of various ranks and stations, our wives, children and helpless old parents, have come to Thee, Sire, to seek justice and protection.

We have become beggars; we are oppressed and burdened by labor beyond our strength; we are humiliated; we are regarded, not as human beings, but as slaves who must endure their bitter fate in silence. . . .

Sire, there are many thousands of us here; we have the appearance of human beings but, in fact, neither we nor the rest of the Russian people enjoy a single human right—not even the right to speak, think, assemble, discuss our needs, or take steps to improve our condition. . . .

Sire! Is this in accordance with God's laws, by the grace of which Thou reignest? . . . Is it better to die—for all of us, the toiling people of all Russia, to die, allowing the capitalists (the exploiters of the working class) and the bureaucrats (who rob the government and plunder the Russian people) to live and enjoy themselves?

This is the choice we face, Sire, and this is why we have come to the walls of Thy palace.

Order these measures and take Thine oath to carry them out. Thou wilt thus make Russia both happy and famous, and Thy name will be engraved in our hearts and in those of our posterity forever. And if Thou dost not so order and dost not respond to our pleas we will die here in this square before Thy palace. We have nowhere else to go and no purpose in going."

1906, more than four hundred mutinies occurred in the military. In the most famous of these, sailors on the battleship *Potemkin* seized control of the ship and executed the officers. Terrorist attacks on police officers and government officials increased. In 1907 shootings and bombings by terrorists took the lives of nearly three thousand people.

Government Response

The tsar and his government, led by Prime Minister Pyotr Stolypin, reacted with force.

Stolypin believed that when harsh measures did not stop unrest, harsher measures should be used. So many people were executed in 1906 and 1907 that the gallows became known as Stolypin's necktie. Despite his toughness, Stolypin realized that the peasants had reason to rebel. To address their concerns, he pushed through reforms to give peasants more land and more individual control over their land. The combination of executions and reforms did bring some peace to the country. The years from 1908 to 1911 were relatively quiet.

The quiet did not last, though. The number of strikes grew quickly in 1912 and 1913. In 1914 nearly half of the indus-

The mutineers from the Potemkin *after their uprising. The sailors rebelled against squalid living conditions and took control of the ship.*

Mutiny on the *Potemkin*

The Potemkin *mutiny of June 1905 began when sailors refused to eat borscht [soup] made with rotten, bug-infested meat. An officer, Commander Giliarovsky, threatened to execute those refusing to eat the soup. According to historian Richard Hough, Giliarovsky was probably bluffing. However Afansay Matushenko took him seriously. Matushenko became a leader of the mutiny. This excerpt is from Hough's book,* The Potemkin Mutiny.

"'Now we'll try again,' began Giliarovsky. . . . 'All those prepared to eat borscht, step forward.'

Again there was a moment of uncertainty, and again the almost apologetic step forward by the older men. Giliarovsky waited, still confident that the presence of the armed guard would this time turn the tide. A few more followed, but not more than fifty in all. His patience was fast draining away, faster than the courage of the men. 'So it's mutiny, is it? . . . All right, we know how to deal with that. If you think there is no discipline in the Navy, then I'll show you how wrong you are. Bosun, bring the ringleaders here.'. . . [About a dozen men were gathered and prepared for execution.]

'Those who will eat their borscht are dismissed. Anyone who remains can see for himself what we do with mutineers in the Navy.'. . .

Matushenko now forced his way toward the front ranks with increased determination, pushing the men aside and calling out to the members of the firing squad. 'Don't shoot your own comrades—you can't kill your own shipmates! Don't fire, comrades!' The appeal rapidly spread, voice rising above voice.

'Get yourselves rifles and ammunition,' came the cries. 'We're taking over the ship.'

With these words, full-scale mutiny had been irrevocably invoked, and nothing could save the *Potemkin* and her officers."

---

trial workers went on strike. Russian cities were almost impossible to govern.

Rasputin

In the midst of the public turmoil, Nicholas II and his wife, Alexandra, faced private troubles that impacted his rule. In 1904 Alexandra had given birth to an heir, Alexis. This wonderful news, though, quickly led to worry. Ten weeks after the birth, the parents learned that Alexis had hemophilia, a blood condition in which the blood does not clot easily. Any small cut or scrape could prove fatal to the young boy. In her worry, Alexandra turned to a religious teacher named Grigory Rasputin. A large, strong peasant from Siberia, Rasputin could barely read and rarely washed. He was an undisciplined man, who was frequently drunk and often led sexual orgies. Yet he had a magnetic personality and a reputation as a faith healer. When Alexandra called Rasputin to the palace, she was immediately convinced of his miraculous powers. He soon became a frequent visitor to the palace.

A Powerful Influence

Indeed, Rasputin did seem able to control the bleeding of young Alexis. Rasputin biographer Joseph Fuhrmann quotes one observer who described the following incident:

> The poor child [Alexis] lay in pain, dark patches under his eyes and his little body all distorted, and the leg terribly swollen. The doctors were just useless . . . more frightened than any of us, . . . whispering among themselves. . . . It was getting late and I was persuaded to go to my rooms. Alicky [the empress Alexandra] then sent a message to Rasputin in St. Petersburg. He reached the palace about midnight or even later. By that time, I had reached my apartments and early in the morning Alicky called me to go to Alexis's room. I just could not believe my eyes. The little boy was not just alive—but well. He was sitting up in bed, the fever gone, the eyes clear and bright, not a sign of any swelling in the leg. Later I learned from Alicky that

Rasputin (pictured), a peasant faith healer, helped Alexandra care for her hemophiliac son, Alexis.

> Rasputin had not even touched the child but merely stood at the foot of the bed and prayed.[96]

Rasputin's power to help Alexis made him Alexandra's most trusted adviser. She asked him about anything that affected her family—which meant everything that affected the tsar and Russia. Through his advice to Alexandra, Rasputin quickly became the most powerful influence on the tsar. To the outraged court nobles, he remained an ignorant, dirty peasant. They detested him but said little for fear of offending Alexandra and the tsar.

Most Russians also disliked Rasputin. His frequent bouts of drunkenness and his participation in sexual orgies offended many Russians. That such an immoral man should be an adviser to the wife of the tsar shocked and angered many Russians.

Regardless of the views of the nobles or the masses, though, Alexandra stood by Rasputin. She believed he had been sent by God to keep her son healthy.

Disaster in World War I

As if these events were not enough to burden the tsar, World War I broke out in Europe in 1914. Peasants signed up for the army, eager to fight on the side of the Allies. In factories making military supplies, strikes and protests stopped. According to writer Harrison Salisbury, "workers on whom the police had fired a fortnight [two weeks] earlier were . . . working day and night without extra pay."[97] Leaders confidently expected the war would be short. Young Russian men dreamed of returning home quickly as heroes. Ward Rutherford says that Nicholas even "issued a ukase [order] changing the name of the capital from the German St. Petersburg to the Russian Petrograd."[98]

But as in Crimea and Manchuria, Russian soldiers went to battle unprepared. They lacked competent leadership, adequate training, and sufficient food. And, most seriously, they lacked guns and ammunition. When the tsar went to visit the troops, he wrote back to his wife, "Half of them have no rifles."[99] Soldiers without guns had poor chances of surviving, let alone winning, battles.

Under these conditions the predictions of quick glory faded fast. The first major battle between Russian and German forces occurred in late August 1914 at Tannenberg, a town one hundred

miles north of the Polish city of Warsaw. The result was a horrible defeat for the Russians. Nearly 170,000 Russians were killed, injured, or captured by the German army. During the first year of fighting, says Lincoln, "nearly three million Russians were killed, wounded, or taken prisoner." And, he adds, "the slaughter continued with no end in sight."[100] Most of the Russian-German battles were in the Polish region of Russia.

As more and more Russians were sent to their deaths, support for the war collapsed. Major General Alfred W. F. Knox was a British officer serving with the Russians. In the autumn of 1916, he noted the fall in morale in his diary:

Tsar Nicholas II, his wife Alexandra, and their son, Alexis. Alexandra had faith that Rasputin could heal Alexis, despite the healer's unpopularity with other Russians.

I hear whispers that the Russian infantry has lost heart and that anti-war propaganda is rife [widespread] in the ranks. It is little wonder that they are downhearted after being driven to the slaughter over the same ground seven times in about a month, and every time taking trenches where their guns could not keep them.[101]

Russians began to wonder what they were dying for. Why had the tsar sent them to fight in these battles in far-off Europe? Lincoln quotes one Russian, who said in 1915: "A Tambov [region southeast of Moscow] peasant is willing to fight to defend the province of Tambov, but a war for Poland, in his opinion, is foreign and useless. The [Tambov] sol-

diers therefore surrender en masse [in large numbers]."[102]

In Russia things were also bad. To produce the ammunition, uniforms, and other supplies for the army meant sacrifices at home. The entire transportation system was tied up with military goods. According to Salisbury, "In the last ten days of January Petrograd got 21 carloads of grain and flour per day instead of the 120 wagons needed to feed the city." One analyst, Mikhail V. Chelnokov, declared "there won't be any bread in February. We have grain for mills that have no fuel, flour where there are no freight cars to haul it and cars where there is no food for the population."[103] As a result of the shortages of food, prices shot upward. Rye flour, wheat flour, potatoes, and meat each cost

at least five times more than they had before the war.

By 1917 more and more Russians wanted out of the war. According to historian Moscow:

The enemy had overrun most of the west and southwest of the country, and two million refugees had to be cared for. Military demands for supplies overburdened the remaining railways. Food and fuel were running short in the cities. Two million soldiers had been killed, and deserters were spreading defeatist talk. Factory workers, stirred by whispered revolutionary propaganda, were restive [impatient]. Grand dukes were considering the ouster of Nicholas and his replacement by his son.[104]

In March 1917 food riots erupted in Petrograd. The government, as it had always done, tried to suppress the uprising but was unsuccessful this time. The Russian soldiers called out to stop the unrest did not fire on the protesters—they joined them. Rather than obey orders from above, they sided with the masses below. The end of Nicholas II's rule was now in sight.

Nicholas II Abdicates

Tsar Nicholas II faced a situation no other tsar had faced. Tsars had ruled during unpopular wars, but never a war as bloody as World War I. Tsars had been unpopular,

Facing widespread opposition and revolts, and lacking military support, Nicholas II was forced to abdicate in 1917.

but never had so many people opposed the entire tsarist system. Tsars had ruled through famines, but never without a strong military to enforce order. And tsars had crushed peasant revolts, but never had a tsar faced massive protests by industrial workers.

The Duma realized that Nicholas II could no longer rule the country. It established a provisional government to rule until elections could be held. A delegation met with the tsar. Given little choice, he abdicated. The 450-year era of tsarist rule of Russia was over.

Russia Since 1917

After Nicholas II abdicated, some Russians urged his brother, Michael, to take his place as tsar. Without some sign of popular support, though, Michael realized that he would not have any real power. He refused to be tsar.

For the next several months Russia was ruled by a provisional, or temporary, government led by Aleksandr Kerensky. Too weak to address the extreme problems facing Russia, the temporary government was overthrown on November 7, 1917, and taken over by a political group called the Bolsheviks. The Bolsheviks were one of several Russian groups that based their political and economic goals on the theories of Karl Marx. Their interpretation of Marx's ideas is a form of socialism that is now called communism. They believed that all businesses should be owned by the government on behalf of the workers in the country. The Bolsheviks hoped their revolution would spark similar uprisings around the world.

The Bolshevik uprising is sometimes called the October Revolution. This name reflects the calendar still used in Russia at the time. It was thirteen days behind the Gregorian calendar in use in Europe and the United States. In 1918 the Bolsheviks adopted the Gregorian calendar.

Bolsheviks in Power

The leader of the Bolsheviks was Nikolay Lenin. He moved quickly to attack the problems facing Russia. Within a year the new government made peace with Germany, ending Russia's part in World War I. It gave land to the peasants and gave workers power to run their factories. It also moved the capital from Petrograd back to Moscow.

The seizure of power by the Bolsheviks, now referred to as the Russian Revolution, marked the start of a three-year civil war in Russia. The Bolsheviks became known as the Reds. Their opponents, the Whites, included a variety of groups united only by their opposition to the Bolsheviks. Some Whites wanted to restore the tsar to power. Others were nobles who wanted to undo the land reforms of the Bolsheviks. Many Whites were socialists who shared Lenin's goals but opposed the Bolsheviks' ruthless, undemocratic methods. According to Henry L. Roberts, the fighting was brutal:

Casualties in the 1917 revolution had been relatively light, but the civil war exacted a fearful toll: battles without prisoners, organized terror and unorganized marauding, Red against White, village against city, nationality against nationality. Entire towns were depopulated. Inevitably, widespread famine followed.[105]

During the fighting the Bolsheviks imprisoned Nicholas II and his family in Ekaterinburg. On July 16, 1918, White forces neared Ekaterinburg. The Bolsheviks feared that the White troops would free the tsar, who would rally support against them. Consequently, the Bolsheviks ordered the execution of the tsar, his wife, and his children. The tsar and his family were only a handful of the thousands of Russians executed during the civil war.

Fearing the spread of communism, countries including Great Britain, France, and the United States supported the Whites. These countries hoped that the Bolsheviks would be defeated and that a new Russian government would rejoin the fight against Germany. To help topple the Bolsheviks, Japan sent seventy-two thousand troops and the United States sent eight thousand troops to invade Russia from the east. Despite these foreign troops, the Reds won the war.

Lenin led the Bolsheviks in overthrowing the government and establishing communism in Russia. The 1917 uprising caused a bloody civil war.

The Soviet Union

In 1922 Russia and its neighbors formed a new country, the Union of Soviet Socialist Republics (USSR), commonly called the Soviet Union. For the next six decades it would be the largest country in the world, covering one-sixth of the world's land area. It included people speaking one hundred different languages. Russia was the largest single republic within the USSR.

Following Lenin's death in 1924, Joseph Stalin became dictator of the Soviet Union. Like Lenin, Stalin claimed to be a Marxist. However, concluded Roberts, the Soviet Union "showed little resemblance to the goals of Marxism."[106] It was not democratic. Workers had little real power to control their workplaces. The government did not allow for civil rights.

Stalin, says Roberts, was "one of the most fearsome rulers of all time."[107] His efforts to bend the country to his will caused tremendous suffering. For example, famine in the 1920s and 1930s was made dramatically worse by the efforts of Stalin to reorganize Soviet agriculture. Six million people died. Later in the 1930s Stalin launched a crackdown on his political opponents. Eight million people were arrested, and about eight hundred thousand of these were executed. Many of the rest were sent to work camps, where they died from hard labor. No tsar had been efficient enough to cause so many deaths. Stalin ruled until his death in 1953.

Stalin's brutal rule did bring significant economic progress. During the 1920s and 1930s the Soviet Union was becoming a powerful, industrialized country. The country made great strides forward in education, health, and equality for women. But like the building of St. Petersburg or the Trans-Siberian Railway, this progress came at tremendous cost to the workers involved.

In 1939 World War II broke out. During most of the war, the Soviets, Great Britain, France, and the United States were allies. They fought against Germany, Italy, and Japan. It was the bloodiest war in human history. Approximately forty million people died. Of these, twenty million were Soviet citizens. In comparison, about half a million U.S. citizens died.

Following World War II the Soviets found themselves in another conflict called the cold war. This time they were rivals with the United States for world leadership. The Soviet Union and the United States did not fight one another directly, but they often supported opposing factions in wars in poor countries. The participation of the Soviet Union and the United States turned minor, local conflicts into larger, more deadly, confrontations. By the 1960s the Soviet Union and the United States were the two most powerful countries in the world.

Return to Russia

In the 1960s and 1970s, Soviet economic growth slowed, and citizens became more and more disillusioned with the communist system. In 1985 Mikhail Gorbachev became leader of the Soviet Union. He pushed a package of economic reforms and reduced the restrictions on individual liberties. Throughout the Soviet Union regions that had once been independent countries demanded a return to independence. Then, in 1991, they began to get it. By the end of the year, with surprisingly little bloodshed, the Soviet Union had dissolved. Once again, Russia became an independent country.

The Significance of Russia's History

Studying Russian history provides an important key to understanding Russia today. The country's 450 years under tsarist rule shaped modern Russia in three important ways. First, Russia is the largest country in the world, even though it no longer controls much of the territory it once did. Russia's size is a result of the persistent expansion of the empire of the tsars. With this expansion came a diverse population, one that included as many non-Russians as it did ethnic Russians by

Under Mikhail Gorbachev, countries within the Soviet Union demanded their independence, and the Soviet Union began to fall apart.

the early 1900s. Russia's great size, which had made it aw power in European affairs since the 1700s, continues to make it an international power.

Second, Russia today is having difficulty developing a democratic political system. This difficulty is partly the result of Russia's long history as a dictatorship under the tsars. For centuries most Russians had no influence on the government of their country. Peasants did not choose the rulers of the country, and any debate of political issues brought the risk of imprisonment or exile. Russians who wanted to change a policy often felt that violence was their only option. Russia's history of brutal repression of dissent has made many Russians skeptical about government. The lack of a history of citizen participation or trust in government has provided a poor foundation for democracy in Russia.

Third, Russia today remains a poor country. Since the 1400s Russia has been poor, despite the hard work of the peasants. Their labor allowed a few nobles and the tsar to lead comfortable lives while they suffered. In addition, whatever wealth Russia produced beyond what was needed to keep people alive was often invested in military ventures. These ventures expanded the empire, but they did not provide a foundation for prosperity. Russia continues to struggle with a legacy of poverty.

Notes

Chapter 1: Emergence of Russia: History Before 1598

1. R. D. Charques, *A Short History of Russia.* New York: E. P. Dutton, 1956, p. 27.

2. Robert Michell and Neville Forbes, trans., *The Chronicle of Novgorod.* London: Offices of the Society, 1914, p. 11.

3. Charques, *A Short History*, p. 25.

4. Melvin C. Wren, *Ancient Russia.* New York: John Day, n.d., p. 122.

5. Quoted in Warren Bartlett Walsh, *Russia and the Soviet Union: A Modern History.* Ann Arbor: University of Michigan Press, 1958, pp. 50–51.

6. "Medieval Russia's Epics, Chronicles, and Tales," by Serge A. Zenkovsky, trans., in Janet G. Vaillant and John Richards II, *From Russia to USSR: A Narrative and Documentary History.* New York: Longman, 1985, pp. 56–57.

7. Joan Hasler, *The Making of Russia.* New York: Delacorte, 1969, p. 29.

8. Geoffrey Barraclough, ed., *The Times Atlas of World History.* Maplewood, NJ: Hammond, 1984, p. 114.

9. Wren, *Ancient Russia*, p. 124.

10. Nicholas V. Riasanovsky, *A History of Russia*, 4th ed. New York: Oxford University Press, 1984, p. 106.

11. Sigismund von Herberstein, *Notes upon Russia: Being a Translation of the Earliest Account of that Country, Entitled Moscoviticarum Commentarii*, R. H. Major, trans. and ed., in Basil Dmytryshyn, ed., *Medieval Russia: A Source Book, 900–1700.* New York: Holt, Rinehart, and Winston, 1967, p. 163.

12. Henry Moscow, *Russia Under the Czars.* New York: Harper & Row, 1962, p. 38.

13. Herberstein, in Dmytryshyn, in *Medieval Russia*, p. 171.

14. Walsh, *Russia and the Soviet Union*, p. 62.

15. James P. Duffy and Vincent L. Ricci, *Czars: Russia's Rulers for over One Thousand Years.* New York: Facts On File, 1995, p. 127.

16. Giles Fletcher, *Russia at the Close of the Sixteenth Century, Comprising the Treatise 'Of the Russe Common Wealth,'* and Edward A. Bond, ed., *The Travels of Sir Jerome Horsey*, in Dmytryshyn, *Medieval Russia*, p. 209.

17. Riasanovsky, *A History of Russia*, p. 151.

18. Quoted in Dmytryshyn, *Medieval Russia*, p. 208.

19. Philip Longworth, *The Cossacks.* New York: Holt, Rinehart, and Winston, 1969, p. 47.

20. E. M. Almedingen, *Land of Muscovy: The History of Early Russia.* New York: Farrar, Straus, and Giroux, 1971, p. 55.

21. Riasanovsky, *A History of Russia*, p. 154.

22. Quoted in Walsh, *Russia and the Soviet Union*, pp. 82–83.

23. Ivar Spector, *An Introduction to Russian History and Culture*, 4th ed. Princeton, NJ: Van Nostrand, 1965, p. 42.

24. V. O. Kliuchevsky, *A Course in Russian History: The Seventeenth Century*, Natalie Duddington, trans. Chicago: Quadrangle Books, 1968, p. 13.

Chapter 2: Growth of an Empire: 1598–1725

25. Almedingen, *Land of Muscovy*, p. 74.

26. Quoted in R. E. F. Smith and David Christian, *Bread and Salt: A Social and Economic History of Food and Drink in Russia.* Cambridge, England: Cambridge University Press, 1984, p. 110.

27. Quoted in Walsh, *Russia and the Soviet Union*, p. 93.

28. W. Bruce Lincoln, *In War's Dark Shadow: The Russians Before the Great War.* New York: Dial Press, 1983, p. 211.

29. Avvakum, *The Life of Archpriest Avvakum, by Himself,* originally translated by Jane Harrison and Hope Mirrlees, London, England: L. Woolf and V. Woolf at the Hogarth Press, 1924; revised translation reprinted in George Vernadsky, sr. ed., *A Source Book for Russian History from Early Times to 1917,* vol. 2. New Haven, CT: Yale University Press, 1972, p. 261.

30. Avvakum, in Vernadsky, *A Source Book,* p. 261.

31. Robert Massie, *Peter the Great: His Life and World.* New York: Knopf, 1980, p. 134.

32. Massie, *Peter the Great,* p. 234.

33. Massie, *Peter the Great,* p. 235.

34. Henri Troyat, *Catherine the Great.* New York: E. P. Dutton, 1980, p. 143.

35. Quoted in Alex de Jonge, *Fire and Water: A Life of Peter the Great.* New York: Coward, McCann, and Geohegan, 1980, p. 102.

36. de Jonge, *Fire and Water,* p. 101.

37. Massie, *Peter the Great,* pp. 360–61.

38. Spector, *An Introduction,* p. 73.

Chapter 3: The Reign of Catherine the Great: 1762–1796

39. Troyat, *Catherine the Great,* p. 146.

40. Virginia Cowles, *The Romanovs.* New York: Harper & Row, 1971, p. 90.

41. Quoted in Troyat, *Catherine the Great,* p. 142.

42. Walsh, *Russia and the Soviet Union,* p. 138.

43. *The Great Reform: Russian Society and the Peasant Problem in the Past and at Present,* A. K. Dzhivelegov, S. P. Melgunov, and V. I. Picheta, eds., Basil Dmytryshyn trans.; in Basil Dmytryshyn, ed., *Imperial Russia: A Source Book, 1700–1917,* 2nd ed. Hinsdale, IL: The Dryden Press, 1973, p. 127.

44. Moscow, *Russia Under the Czars,* pp. 88–89.

45. Quoted in Troyat, *Catherine the Great,* p. 213.

46. Michael T. Florinsky, *Russia: A History and an Interpretation,* vol. 1. New York: Macmillan, 1953, p. 591.

47. Troyat, *Catherine the Great,* p. 214.

Chapter 4: Russia's Resistance to Change: 1796–1856

48. Quoted in Walsh, *Russia and the Soviet Union,* p. 165.

49. Charques, *A Short History,* p. 153.

50. Quoted in Walsh, *Russia and the Soviet Union,* p. 170.

51. Florinsky, *Russia,* p. 254.

52. Felix Markham, *Napoleon.* New York: Mentor, 1963, p. 194.

53. Quoted in Eugene Tarle, *Napoleon's Invasion of Russia, 1812.* New York: Oxford University Press, 1942, p. 211.

54. Tarle, *Napoleon's Invasion of Russia, 1812,* pp. 213–14.

55. Markham, *Napoleon,* p. 196.

56. Quoted in Walsh, *Russia and the Soviet Union,* p. 186.

57. Edward Crankshaw, *The Shadow of the Winter Palace: Russia's Drift to Revolution, 1825–1917.* New York: Viking, 1976, p. 13.

58. Crankshaw, *The Shadow,* p. 14.

59. Quoted in Cowles, *The Romanovs,* p. 158.

60. Crankshaw, *The Shadow,* p. 17.

61. Charques, *A Short History,* p. 171.

62. Charques, *A Short History,* p. 170.

63. Cowles, *The Romanovs,* p. 160.

64. Quoted in Walsh, *Russia and the Soviet Union,* p. 187.

65. Colin White, *Russia and America: The Roots of Economic Divergence.* London: Croom Helm, 1987, p. 135.

66. Isaiah Berlin, *Russian Thinkers.* New York: Viking, 1978, p. 208.

67. Cowles, *The Romanovs,* p. 178.

68. Quoted in Crankshaw, *The Shadow,* pp. 139–40.

69. Florinsky, *Russia,* p. 299.

Chapter 5: Reform and Reaction: 1856–1894

70. Crankshaw, *The Shadow,* p. 157.

71. Quoted in Florinsky, *Russia,* p. 301.

72. Quoted in Walsh, *Russia and the Soviet Union*, p. 252.

73. Peter Kropotkin, *Memoirs of a Revolutionist*, in Vernadsky, *A Source Book*, vol. 3, p. 604.

74. Vaillant and Richards, *From Russia to USSR*, p. 86.

75. Quoted in Peter Lyaschenko, *History of the National Economy of Russia*. L. M. Herman, trans. New York: Macmillan, 1949, p. 374.

76 Berlin, *Russian Thinkers*, p. 216.

77. Avrahm Yarmolinsky, *Road to Revolution*. New York: Collier, 1962, p. 189.

78. Moscow, *Russia Under the Czars*, p. 103.

79. Chaim Weizmann, *Trial and Error: The Autobiography of Chaim Weizmann*. New York: Schocken Books, 1949, pp. 18, 19.

80. S. D. Urusov, *Memoirs of a Russian Governor, Prince S. D. Urusov*, Herman Rosenthal, trans., in Vernadsky, *A Source Book*, vol. 3, p. 699.

81. Quoted in Crankshaw, *The Shadow*, p. 282.

82. Lincoln, *In War's Dark Shadow*, p. 220.

83. Quoted in A. M. Gudvan, *Essays on the History of the Movement of Sales-Clerical Workers in Russia*, in Victoria E. Bonnell, ed., *The Russian Worker: Life and Labor Under the Tsarist Regime*. Berkeley: University of California Press, 1983, p. 192.

84. Kyril Fitzlyon and Tatiana Browning, *Before the Revolution: A View of Russia Under the Last Tsar*. Woodstock, NY: Overlook Press, 1978, p. 36.

85. Quoted in Lincoln, *In War's Dark Shadow*, p. 13.

86. Quoted in Lincoln, *In War's Dark Shadow*, p. 27.

87. Lincoln, *In War's Dark Shadow*, p. 24.

Chapter 6: The End of Tsarist Rule: 1894–1917

88. Quoted in Fitzlyon and Browning, *Before the Revolution*, p. 15.

89. Quoted in Crankshaw, *The Shadow*, pp. 311–12.

90. Quoted in Harrison E. Salisbury, *Black Night, White Snow: Russia's Revolutions, 1905–1917*. Garden City, NY: Doubleday, 1978, p. 94.

91. Walsh, *Russia and the Soviet Union*, p. 320.

92. Moscow, *Russia Under the Czars*, p. 107.

93. Quoted in Walsh, *Russia and the Soviet Union*, p. 331.

94. Quoted in Salisbury, *Black Night, White Snow*, p. 128.

95. Lincoln, *In War's Dark Shadow*, p. 295.

96. Quoted in Joseph T. Fuhrmann, *Rasputin: A Life*. New York: Praeger, 1990, p. 27.

97. Salisbury, *Black Night, White Snow*, p. 252.

98. Ward Rutherford, *The Russian Army in World War I*. London: Gordon Cremonesi, 1975, p. 6.

99. Quoted in Walsh, *Russia and the Soviet Union*, p. 363.

100. Lincoln, *In War's Dark Shadow*, p. 443.

101. Alfred W. F. Knox, *With the Russian Army, 1914–1917*. New York: Arno, 1971, p. 488.

102. Quoted in Lincoln, *In War's Dark Shadow*, p. 435.

103. Quoted in Salisbury, *Black Night, White Snow*, pp. 321–22.

104. Moscow, *Russia Under the Czars*, pp. 110–11.

Epilogue: Russia Since 1917

105. Henry L. Roberts, "The Russian Revolution and the Stalin Era," in John A. Garraty and Peter Gay, eds., *The Columbia History of the World*. New York: Harper & Row, 1972, p. 999.

106. Roberts, in Garraty and Gay, *The Columbia History of the World*, p. 1,003.

107. Roberts, in Garraty and Gay, *The Columbia History of the World*, p. 1,004.

For Further Reading

Aleksandr Afanas'ev, *Russian Fairy Tales.* New York: Pantheon Books, 1945. Norbert Guterman, trans. A large collection of traditional Russian stories reflecting the values and beliefs of Russian peasants.

E. M. Almedingen, *Catherine: Empress of Russia.* New York: Dodd, Mead, and Company. 1961. A well-researched, graceful biography of Catherine the Great.

———, *Land of Muscovy: The History of Early Russia.* New York: Farrar, Straus, and Giroux, 1971. A readable look at early Russian history.

Victoria E. Bonnell, ed., *The Russian Worker: Life and Labor Under the Tsarist Regime.* Berkeley: University of California Press, 1983. Excellent primary sources in engaging translations that give the flavor of life in Russia in the late 1800s and early 1900s.

Virginia Cowles, *The Romanovs.* New York: Harper & Row, 1971. A superb selection of anecdotes, quotations, and artwork about the tsars, beginning with the first Romanov, Michael, who took power in 1613.

Marquis de Custine, *Journey for Our Time: The Russian Journals of the Marquis de Custine.* Phyllis Penn Kohler, ed. and trans. Chicago: n. p. 1951. This edition of a French visitor's journey through Russia in 1839 provides fascinating glimpses into Russian life and is usually easy to read.

Kyril Fitzlyon and Tatiana Browning, *Before the Revolution: A View of Russia Under the Last Tsar.* Woodstock, NY: Overlook Press, 1978. An excellent collection of photographs combined with a perceptive essay about everyday life in Russia in the late 1800s and early 1900s.

Joan Hasler, *The Making of Russia.* New York: Delacorte, 1969. A well-written survey of Russian history that includes several fine primary-source excerpts and good coverage of geography.

W. Bruce Lincoln, *In War's Dark Shadow: The Russians Before the Great War.* New York: Dial Press, 1983. A first-rate example of a scholarly book for a general audience. Though written for adults, the engaging style will make it accessible to interested younger readers.

Henry Moscow, *Russia Under the Czars.* New York: Harper & Row, 1962. A short, spirited survey of Russian history that provides an excellent introduction to the topic for general readers.

Tamara Talbot Rice, *Finding Out About the Early Russians.* New York: Lothrop, Lee, and Shepard, 1964. An anecdotal look at ancient Russian history written for young readers.

Harrison E. Salisbury, *Black Night, White Snow: Russia's Revolutions, 1905–1917.* Garden City, NY: Doubleday, 1978. A long but lively book filled with stories written by a prominent journalist from the United States.

Melvin C. Wren, *Ancient Russia.* New York: John Day n. d. A scholarly yet readable book on the early period in Russian history.

Additional Works Consulted

Geoffrey Barraclough, ed., *The Times Atlas of World History*. Maplewood, NJ: Hammond, 1984. Contains over 600 maps covering important events, movements, and empires from the origins of humanity to the 1980s.

Isaiah Berlin, *Russian Thinkers*. New York: Viking, 1978. A collection of writings by one of Great Britain's most respected students of Russian culture.

Jerome Blum, *Lord and Peasant in Russia from the Ninth to the Nineteenth Century*. Princeton, NJ: Princeton University Press, 1961. A highly regarded analysis of economic and social relationships in Russia.

John Carey, ed., *Eyewitness to History*. Cambridge, MA: Harvard University Press, 1987. This collection of firsthand accounts of historical events includes Baron de Méneval's account of the French invasion of Russia in 1812.

R. D. Charques, *A Short History of Russia*. New York: E. P. Dutton, 1956. A challenging book filled with provocative judgments about events in Russian history and excellent personality profiles.

Edward Crankshaw, *The Shadow of the Winter Palace: Russia's Drift to Revolution, 1825–1917*. New York: Viking, 1976. An engaging overview of the long path leading from the Decembrist Revolt to the Bolshevik Revolution.

W. P. Cresson, *The Cossacks: Their History and Country*. New York: Brentano, 1919. A classic account of one of Russia's most intriguing groups.

Vincent Cronin, *Catherine: Empress of All the Russias*. New York: William Morrow, 1978. A solid biography of Catherine the Great.

Alex de Jonge, *Fire and Water: A Life of Peter the Great*. New York: Coward, McCann, and Geohegan, 1980. A nicely written one-volume study of Peter the Great.

Basil Dmytryshyn, ed., *Imperial Russia: A Source Book, 1700–1917*. 2nd ed. Hinsdale, IL: The Dryden Press, 1973. A collection of primary sources on Russian history in the two centuries prior to the 1917 revolution.

————, *Medieval Russia: A Source Book, 900–1700*. New York: Holt, Rinehart, and Winston, 1967. A fine collection of primary sources. Particularly useful for the extensive excerpts from accounts by visitors to Russia and for its readable translations of older documents.

James P. Duffy and Vincent L. Ricci, *Czars: Russia's Rulers for over One Thousand Years*. New York: Facts On File, 1995. An engaging history of Russia as seen through the biographies of its leaders.

Barbara Engel, "Women, Work and Family in the Factories of Rural Russia," *Russian History*, vol. 16, nos. 2–4, 1989. A fascinating look at how industrialization affected women in Russia.

Michael T. Florinsky, *Russia: A History and an Interpretation*. Vol. 1. New York: Macmillan, 1953. A detailed account most useful for in-depth study of Russian history.

Joseph T. Fuhrman, *Rasputin: A Life.* New York: Praeger, 1990. A biography of one of Russia's most enigmatic characters.

Richard Hough, *The Potemkin Mutiny.* New York: Pantheon, 1961. A dramatic, colorful account of the most famous mutiny in Russian history.

Daniel H. Kaiser and Gary Marker, *Reinterpreting Russian History: Readings, 860–1860s.* New York: Oxford University Press, 1994. A recent collection of primary and secondary sources that provides more coverage of social history than do earlier collections.

V. O. Kliuchevsky, *A Course in Russian History: The Seventeenth Century.* Natalie Duddington, trans. Chicago: Quadrangle Books, 1968. A fine translation of a perceptive work by a great historian.

———*A History of Russia.* C. J. Hogarth, trans. New York: Russell and Russell, 1960. A classic interpretation of Russian history by one of Russia's most respected historians.

Alfred W. F. Knox, *With the Russian Army, 1914–1917.* New York: Arno, 1971. An insider's account of life in the Russian army during World War I.

Peter Kolchin, *Unfree Labor: American Slavery and Russian Serfdom.* Cambridge, MA: Belknap Press, 1987. A brilliant comparative study of the parallel but distinct institutions that shaped much of Russian and American history.

James H. Krukones, "Satan's Blood, Tsar's Ink: Rural Alcoholism in an Official 'Publication for the People,' 1881–1917," *Russian History*, vol. 18, no. 4, 1991. Quotation from *Village Herald*, October 27, 1881.

Philip Longworth, *The Cossacks.* New York: Holt, Rinehart, and Winston, 1969. A survey of the history and culture of the Cossacks.

Peter Lyaschenko, *History of the National Economy of Russia.* L. M. Herman, trans. New York: Macmillan, 1949. The standard account of Russian economic development by a prominent Russian scholar.

Felix Markham, *Napoleon.* New York: Mentor, 1963. An excellent one-volume biography of France's powerful dictator.

Robert Massie, *Peter the Great: His Life and World.* New York: Knopf, 1980. A highly acclaimed work about the most significant and controversial tsar in Russian history.

Claude-François de Méneval, *Memoirs to Serve for the History of Napoleon I.* R. H. Sherard, trans. Paris: E. Dentu, 1894.

Robert Michell and Neville Forbes, trans. *The Chronicle of Novgorod.* London: Office of the Society, 1914. A translation of one of the most important sources in medieval Russian history.

Bernard Pares, *A History of Russia.* New York: Knopf, 1948. 5th ed. This book was the standard one-volume history of Russia for much of the twentieth century.

John Perry, *The State of Russia Under the Present Czar.* New York: Da Capo Press, 1968. A reprint of a 1716 book by an insightful visitor to Russia.

Nicholas V. Riasanovsky, *A History of Russia.* 4th ed. New York: Oxford University Press, 1984. A comprehensive, serious survey of Russian history that makes an excellent resource book.

Henry L. Roberts, "The Russian Revolution and the Stalin Era," in John A. Garraty and Peter Gay, eds., *The Columbia History of the World*. New York: Harper & Row, 1972. A brief account of modern Russian history.

Ward Rutherford, *The Russian Army in World War I*. London: Gordon Cremonesi, 1975. A study of Russia's military role in World War I.

R. E. F. Smith and David Christian, *Bread and Salt: A Social and Economic History of Food and Drink in Russia*. Cambridge, England: Cambridge University Press, 1984. A scholarly work that provides fascinating details and analyses of what Russians have eaten over the centuries and why.

Ivar Spector, *An Introduction to Russian History and Culture*. 4th ed. Princeton, NJ: Van Nostrand, 1965. A solid overview of life in Russia.

Eugene Tarle, *Napoleon's Invasion of Russia, 1812*. New York: Oxford University Press, 1942. A brilliant description and analysis of one of Russia's greatest military victories.

Henri Troyat, *Catherine the Great*. New York: E. P. Dutton, 1980. A well-written, detailed biography by a well-respected writer.

Janet G. Vaillant and John Richards II, *From Russia to USSR: A Narrative and Documentary History*. New York: Longman, 1985. A combination of excerpts from primary and secondary sources that provides a good survey of Russian history.

George Vernadsky, sr. ed., *A Source Book for Russian History from Early Times to 1917*.

3 vols. New Haven, CT: Yale University Press, 1972. A large collection of primary sources, including many documents not easily available elsewhere.

Dimitri von Mohrenschildt, *The Russian Revolution of 1917: Contemporary Accounts*. New York: Oxford University Press, 1971. A collection of sources on the 1917 revolution from people who lived through it.

Warren Bartlett Walsh, *Russia and the Soviet Union: A Modern History*. Ann Arbor: University of Michigan Press, 1958. A well-written scholarly survey of Russian history that includes a good mixture of anecdotes and primary sources, as well as comments on various interpretations of Russian history.

Warren B. Walsh, ed., *Readings in Russian History*. Vol. 1. Syracuse, NY: Syracuse University Press, 1963. A collection of primary and secondary sources, including many excerpts from historians.

Chaim Weizmann, *Trial and Error: The Autobiography of Chaim Weizmann*. New York: Shocken Books, 1949. The life story of Israel's first president, including his childhood in Russia.

Colin White, *Russia and America: The Roots of Economic Divergence*. London: Croom Helm, 1987. A provocative comparison of the two countries that dominated much of the twentieth century.

Avrahm Yarmolinsky, *Road to Revolution*. New York: Collier, 1962. An engaging account of the development of Russian revolutionary thought prior to 1917.

Index

Alexander I
  conservatism of, 44
  death of, 47
  war with France, 45–47
Alexander II
  assassination of, 61
  Crimean War and, 56
  emancipation of serfs by, 57–59
  reforms of, 58
Alexander III
  assassination plot against, 61
  death of, 70
  famine during reign of, 69
  industrialization and, 65–66, 68
  Jews and, 62–65
  trade and, 68–69
Alexandra (wife of Nicholas II), 75–77
Alexis
  expands Russia, 25–27
  Jews and, 27
  reforms Orthodox Church, 27–30
Alexis (son of Nicholas II), 75–76
anti-Semitism, 27, 62–65
army, Russian
  development of, 16
  during Crimean War, 55–56
  during Napoleonic War, 45–47
during Russo-Japanese War, 71, 72
during World War I, 77–78, 79
revolt against Nicholas I and, 49–50
under Peter the Great, 31, 32, 34–35
Austria, 37
Avvakum (archpriest), 29–30

barschina (labor tax), 41
Bell (journal), 53
Bloody Sunday, 71, 72
Bolsheviks, 80–81
Borodin, Aleksandr, 53
Borodino, Battle of, 46
Bund movement, 65

capitalism, 54, 66
Catherine II (the Great)
  characteristics of, 36
  death of, 44
  foreign policy of, 36–37
  influenced by western Europe, 37–38
  peasants and, 38–39, 41–43
censorship, 52–53
Chekhov, Anton, 53
Chernyshevsky, N. G., 55
Chronicle of Novgorod, The, 12–13
civil war, 80–81
cold war, 82
Constantine (brother of Nicholas I), 48–49
Cossacks, 25, 34
Crimea, 37
Crimean War, 55–56
Custine, marquis de, 45

Decembrists, 71
  revolt of, 49–51
democracy, 70
  in Novgorod, 17–18
  intellectuals work for, 53, 59–60
Diderot, Denis, 37–38
Dmitri (half-brother of Fyodor), 24
Domostroy (household manual), 16
Dostoyevsky, Fyodor, 53
Duma (legislature), 72, 79

Ekaterinburg, 81
Enlightenment, 37–38

factory workers, 11, 66, 67
famines, 12–13, 23, 69
Fletcher, Giles
  on Ivan IV, 19
  on Russian customs, 21
folk tales, 43, 51
France, 44–47, 48
Fyodor (son of Ivan IV), 23
Fyodor III, 30

Genghis Khan, 15–16

Germany, 77, 80
Glinka, Mikhail, 53
Godunov, Boris, 23–24
Golden Horde, 15–17
Gorbachev, Mikhail, 82
Great Northern War,
    34–35
Grozny, 19, 21
    see also Ivan IV (the
        Terrible)

hemophilia, 75, 76
Herberstein, Sigismund
    von
    on capture of Novgorod,
        17
    on judicial system, 18
    on women, 13
Herzen, Aleksandr
    followers of, 59–60
    on capitalism, 53–54, 66
    on Decembrist Revolt,
        51
    on emancipation of
        serfs, 58

Industrial Revolution, 52,
    65–68
intellectuals, 53–55, 59–60,
    72
Ivan III (the Great), 17–19
Ivan IV (the Terrible),
    19–21, 22

Japan, 70–71, 72–73, 81
Jews, 37
    self-defense of, 64
    under Alexander III,
        62–65
    under Alexis, 27

Kerensky, Aleksandr, 80
Khomyakov, A. S., 55
Kiev, 12, 25, 50
Kievan Russia, 12–15
Kishinev, 63–65
Knox, Alfred W. F., 77–78
Kossuth, Lajos, 55
Kropotkin, Pyotr, 58
Kutuzov (Russian officer),
    46

Lenin, Nikolay, 61, 80, 81
Lithuania, 37
Little Mother. *See*
    Catherine II (the Great)

Marx, Karl, 60, 80
Marxism, 81
Matushenko, Afansay, 75
Méneval, Claude-François
    de, 48
Michael (brother of
    Nicholas II), 80
Mongols, 15–17
Moscow, 10, 24, 25, 45, 80
    captured by French,
        46–47, 48
    princes of, 17, 26

Napoleon Bonaparte,
    44–48
Narva, Battle of, 34–35
Nicholas I, 48, 49
    army revolt against,
        49–50
    creates police state, 50
    Crimean War and, 55–56
    death of, 56
    economic development
        under, 51–52

Nicholas II
    abdication of, 79
    coronation of, 70
    execution of, 81
    protests during reign of,
        70, 71–72, 73–75
    reforms of, 72, 74
    Russo-Japanese War and,
        70–71, 72–73
    World War I and, 77–79
Nihilists, 55
Nikon (patriarch), 29–30
nobles, 10–11
    characteristics of, 30
    under Boris Godunov,
        23–24
    under Catherine II, 39,
        41
    under Ivan IV, 19–20
    under Michael
        Romanov, 24–25, 26
"Notes upon Russia"
    (Herberstein), 13
Novgorod, 12–13, 17–18,
    25

obrok (tax), 39, 41
October Revolution, 80
Old Believers, 29, 42
Oprichniki (police force),
    20
Orthodox Church
    development of Russian
        identity and, 15
    foreign relations and,
        14–15, 25
    reforms under Alexis,
        27–30
    Russification and, 61–62,
        63

under Mongols, 16

Paul (son of Catherine II), 44
peasants, 11, 51
    become serfs, 19, 21–22
    conservatism of, 30, 39, 54, 60
    diet of, 40
    during Industrial Revolution, 66, 67
    during 1800s, 52
    emancipation of, 57–59
    famine and, 69
    health of, 39
    in Kievan Russia, 12–14
    life of, 12–14
    Pugachov's uprising, 41–43
    reaction to radicals, 60
    religion of, 14
    state, 21–22
People's Will, 60–61
Peter II, 36
Peter the Great
    builds St. Petersburg, 35
    characteristics of, 31
    childhood of, 31
    death of, 35
    expands Russia, 34–35
    influenced by western Europe, 31
    peasants and, 35
    reforms of, 31–35
Petrograd, 77, 79, 80
Plekhanov, Georgy, 60
Pogodin, Mikhail P., 33
pogroms, 63–65
Poland, 14, 24, 25, 37
political terrorism, 60–61

Potemkin mutiny, 74, 75
princes of Moscow, 17, 26
protests, 70, 71–72, 73–75
Prussia, 37
Pugachov, Yemelyan, 41–43
Pushkin, Aleksandr, 52–53

radicals (of 1873–1874), 59–61
railroads, 66, 68
Rasputin, Grigory, 76–77
Reds, 80–81
Rimsky-Korsakov, Nikolay, 53
Roman Catholicism, 14, 24, 25
Romanov, Michael, 24–25, 26
Romanov, Philaret, 25
Russia
    independence of, 82
    peoples of
        customs of, 21
        ethnic, 10
        nonethnic, 10, 27, 37, 42, 61–65
    size of, 10
Russian Empire, 12–15
Russian Orthodoxy. See Orthodox Church
Russian Revolution, 80–81
Russification, 61–65
Russo-Japanese War, 70–71, 72–73

serfs. See peasants
Siberia, 20, 28, 57
    peoples of, 27
    prison camps in, 26, 29, 68

railway across, 66, 68
resources of, 20, 26, 68
slavery, 12
Slavophiles, 54–55
Slavs, 10, 12, 15
socialism, 54, 65, 80
Soviet Union, 81–82
Stalin, Joseph, 81–82
St. George's Day, 19
Stolypin, Pyotr, 74
St. Petersburg
    becomes Petrograd, 77
    Bloody Sunday, 71, 72
    building of, 35
    Decembrist Revolt in, 49–50
Stravinsky, Igor, 53
strikes, 70, 71–72, 73, 74–75
Sweden, 37
    invasion of Russia by, 24
    treaty with Russia (1617), 25
    war with Russia (1700–1721), 34–35

Tannenberg, Poland, 77
Tatars (Tartars), 12, 15–16, 25
taxes
    under Catherine II, 39, 41
    under Ivan IV, 20
    under Peter the Great, 35
    see also tribute
Tchaikovsky, Pyotr (Peter), 53
terrorism, political, 60–61
Time of Troubles, 23–24, 25

Tolstoy, Leo, 53
  on conservatism of
    peasants, 54
  on Crimean War, 56
torture, use of, 32
trade
  in Kievan Russia, 12
  under Alexander III,
    68–69
  under Mongols, 17
  under Nicholas I, 51–52
Trans-Siberian Railway, 66,
  68
tribute
  in Kievan Russia, 12
  under Mongols, 16, 17
Tsar Liberator. *See*
  Alexander II
tsars
  absolute power of, 10,
    22, 26, 35, 41, 44, 45,
    49, 70

beginning of rule of, 19
end of rule of, 79
legacy of, 82–83
Turkey, 34, 37

Ukraine, 25, 37
Ulyanov, Aleksandr, 61, 63
  see also Lenin, Nikolay
Ulyanov, Vladimir, 61
Union of Soviet Socialist
  Republics (USSR),
  81–82
United States, 58, 59, 81,
  82
university students, 11
Uvarov, Ivan, 28

Vasily (son of Ivan III), 19
Vladimir (Kievan ruler),
  14
Voltaire, 37–38, 41
Vyshnegradskii, Ivan, 69

Weizmann, Chaim, 62, 64
Westerners, 53–55, 59–60
Whites (political party),
  80–81
Winter Palace, 71, 73
women
  during Industrial
    Revolution, 66, 67
  in 1500s, 13
  use of cosmetics by, 21
World War I, 15
  army during, 77–78, 79
  peace with Germany, 80
  shortages during, 77–78
  support for, 77–78, 79
World War II, 82
writers, Russian, 52–53

Yermak Timofeyevich, 20,
  25

Picture Credits

About the Author

James E. Strickler has helped write and edit numerous elementary and high school textbooks in history, economics, government, geography, English, science, and mathematics. Raised in Grinnell, Iowa, he received a B.A. from Grinnell College and an M.A.T. from the University of Chicago. He now lives in Chicago with his wife and two children.